SUSIE RA

C000183262

BE THE LEADER YOU WANT TO SEE

Reveal your talents, create fulfilment and
confidently step into the career you were made for

R3THINK PRESS

First published in Great Britain in 2020
by Rethink Press (www.rethinkpress.com)

Credits

Cover image © klesign | Adobe Stock
Question mark by Miroku Sama from the Noun Project
Heart by Christian Baptist from the Noun Project
Speedometer by Nociconist from the Noun Project

Author photograph by http://nikkibowling.com

Praise

'Wow! I've read a lot of self-help books, but this one is a game-changer. It is frank, pragmatic, and will change your life! You will get the answers you've been searching for and craving from this book. If you want to make an enormous leap, buy this book. I couldn't read it quickly enough.'
— **Nikki Peterson**, Commercial Director, *Psychologies* magazine

'Empowering. Susie's no-nonsense, intelligent approach encourages us to take responsibility for our lives and gives practical steps for getting to the life we ultimately want to lead. This book is honest and kind, like the advice of a good friend.'
— **Orla Chennaoui**, Sports Presenter, Eurosport

'We all need that person who challenges us to stop making excuses. Some of my greatest supporters have simply refused to listen to my reasons not to take action. Susie acknowledges all those fears, and gives you the tools to recognise them and the nudge of encouragement to take the brave step past them towards your next destination. I highly recommend this book for women looking for a low-risk way to transform their careers.'
— **Clare Mortimer**, Executive Partner, IBM

'A veritable treasure trove of actionable advice to reclaim your confidence, reveal what brings you joy and recalibrate your inner compass. Susie writes from experience; the examples sprinkled like fairy dust throughout the book substantiate her insights. If you are in need of a map that guides you away from what no longer serves you and focuses you on the areas with the greatest impact, then you need to devour this book *now!*'
— **Sarah Cairns**, Freelance Digital Transformation Consultant

'Totally recommended: five stars from me. Packed to the brim with tips and tricks to help you achieve your goals and thrive in your career.'
— **Vanessa Vallely**, OBE, Managing Director, WeAreTheCity

'The perfect book to pivot when the rug has been pulled from under you. Each chapter is like having a one-on-one coaching conversation specifically crafted to be your shortcut to success. I felt more confident by the end of the book knowing how to leverage what I already have. Filled with practical advice, tips and impactful stories, and interwoven with Susie's own beautifully written career journey, this book will be one you re-read every year.'
— **Galia Gil**, Authentic Leadership Programme lead, IBM

'I feel utterly moved. This book speaks to the heart. Susie eloquently captures how we self-inflict pain and put obstacles in the way of our personal growth. I could hear her talking to me as she delivers such simple, practical and actionable steps with clarity. This book is an indispensable companion packed full with so many lightbulb moments. It's unfathomably brilliant, a gift of a read. Buy it for the women on your team. No, buy it for every woman you know!'
— **Kate Kempe**, Senior Manager, Amazon

To my daughter, Elise. I dedicate this book and almost everything I put my heart into, to you, my muse. You are the most fun, supportive, loving, honest and brilliant human being I know. The difference I hope to make with this book is just a drop in the ocean compared with the impact you will make one day. You are the future, and you make me so proud. The kindness in your heart and the wideness of your eyes is like heaven to me. I love you more than I could ever capture on these pages. I hope I continue to be the leader you want to see.

Contents

Foreword

There has never been a better time to be a woman and never a better time to take the lead as a woman in business. Not only because women are the changemakers, the ones who are taking up their cause for themselves and future generations, but also because it is clear that there is a dawning realisation that diverse teams make better business decisions and drive better outcomes. Business needs more women in leadership positions.

So how do you get yourself to the top table? Sometimes there are skills that you need but much of the time it is simply a matter of reframing your thinking and showing up as the best possible version of yourself. If you are battling with how to get to the top of your career, if you are concerned about what it is going to take to be successful, this book is for you.

I first met Susie when we shared a stage for Ada Lovelace Day. We hit it off instantly, with a mutual passion for using our experience to support the sisterhood, celebrate diversity, advocate for inclusive behaviour and drive for equality. Her easy, if sometimes provocative, style comes across on every page of this book. It feels like you are sharing an everyday chat about leadership that is nudging you forwards and offering both the challenge and the kindness needed in equal measure.

Not only is Susie an accomplished coach, her real genius is in observing those tiny inflection points that shape our behaviour. She takes these observations and nudges us towards breakthrough moments that change lives and throw up different perspectives, so that previously insoluble situations suddenly hold new possibility. It is as much an art as a science, which she deploys like a laser every time she engages.

In my work, I come across many women joining and struggling to climb or stay on the career ladder; they will all benefit from this advice. Importantly, there is an opportunity for those women with significant experience who feel pigeonholed, stuck and confused about the next step. You will find clarity in these pages and easy and practical words of encouragement to embrace who you are and leverage it to create the career you want.

No doubt, there have been pivotal moments in your professional life, as there have been in mine. The moment I was rejected for a position that I was perfectly qualified for just because they 'simply did not put women on the leadership team' was a bitter pill to swallow, but I found myself reframing it as an opportunity to 'look for the miracle'. What could I learn from this experience? I decided that it was, at least, a good thing that he had told me; if I had worked there another five years and not known about the unwritten rule, I think I really would have been distraught! So I found myself a role as managing director of a global software company and never looked back. Reframing experiences like this is beautifully covered in Part Two of this book, and I can tell you that changing perspectives is a useful and nurturing tool to have in your kitbag.

Of course, you can experience imbalance and unfairness whether you identify as a man or a woman in business. This book is aimed at women so that we can stop talking about including women through quotas and start being inundated with their applications and desire to get involved!

The barriers that we think stand in our way may not actually be in the way. You don't necessarily need more knowledge or skills to be at the top. You may have a self-limiting belief or a 'story' you tell yourself that stops you getting there. My coping mechanism for my first role as a managing director was to avoid offering solutions and to be constantly curious, to ask questions about everything. That way I couldn't run out of answers! Plus, I learned a lot very fast. Once I let go of needing to know everything, I felt free and surrounded by competent people who felt they had the space to contribute. Learning the ability to question as a way of coping with your own fears of inadequacy makes you interested versus interesting. Through this book, Susie will take you on this journey.

It is important to find your own way. Let this book be your guide. Susie breaks this book down into three simple parts, which cover understanding how you operate, developing the courage to be the best version of yourself and then marketing that to the world in a way that creates impact and opportunity.

Stand your ground and own the space that you command. Use this book to turn the volume up on your voice and to maximise your impact. Diverse teams really matter and are needed more now than ever to break the currency of 'hide it, keep it and don't share it', to promoting a culture of openness, tolerance and a celebration of differences. If we are to thrive in a digital future, we must ensure that all of our voices are heard. If we don't, we risk creating a world for the few and not for the many.

If you're serious about making an impact in a way that ignites the best in you, this book is required reading.

Jacqueline de Rojas, CBE

Jacqueline is President of techUK and co-chair of the Board Institute of Coding. She is an advisor and non-executive director on several plc boards, as well as a business mentor at the Merryck Group. She is passionate about diversity and inclusion in all its forms, which informs the support she lends at @TheYouthGroupHQ, @accelerate-Her, and the @girlguiding, The Guide Association.

Jacqueline was awarded a CBE for Services to International Trade in Technology in the Queen's New Year Honours list 2018.

Introduction

When you have big goals, goals you haven't achieved before, you sometimes need to be forced into action by something you have a strong opinion about. I was on the panel at Women In Sport in 2018 and heard a phrase that I hadn't heard before: 'You can't be what you can't see.' I instantly got that uneasy feeling in my stomach that I get when I want to reject something.

I have a strong leaning towards that which is helpful, and, in my view, this phrase was simply not. What a disempowering thing to believe. As if there aren't enough reasons for women to remain somewhat invisible in the workplace. Now there is a phrase confirming that there aren't enough role models and giving us licence to play small. To settle. To wait for someone else to set an example we can be inspired by.

I have a fundamental problem with that. It gave me the nudge I needed to write a book on personal growth, one that I felt hadn't been written yet, and certainly not with the anecdotes and stories that have worked so beautifully with my clients. I want to stop the hundreds of thousands of women who are capable and brilliant from getting in their own way. And I want them to stop believing that having a successful and fulfilling career that truly makes an impact requires them to compromise their identity.

The jobs that we have a thirst for are available to those people who get in the game and choose to play out of their skin. While this is an exciting notion, I know that so many women will 'Yes, but' themselves out of taking action. They will buy into all the reasons they can't act, instead of seeing all the possible ways that they may be able to.

This book will show you the personal cost of shrinking to fit your current story. It will help you to think and aim bigger, and give you specific, manageable actions to change how you show up, so that you can truly make an impact – maybe even leave a legacy.

I've worked with hundreds of women just like you, who entertain lofty thoughts, but get dragged back into the weeds when they wonder how they have been working this hard for so long, and yet feel that effort has not brought them the career they'd love. The answer is that you have committed your thinking and your time to things that don't move your needle. Painful to hear perhaps, but a relief when I tell you how you can apply your efforts in a more targeted way, which will not only help your career surge, but will leave you with better relationships than you could ever have imagined.

Contrary to common belief, getting to the top of your game doesn't have to spell personal sacrifice. In this new age, the person who is the most connected and balanced personally is the one who will profit professionally.

Like every female client I have ever had, you seem to be waiting for something to change. It won't. Not until *you* do. You need to decide that the time for that change to happen is now.

This book is for professional women like you, who are highly capable but whose talents are being wasted in their comfort zone. Your time is spent running and re-running the same soundtrack of self-doubt, which only serves to frustrate you – it will not move you forward.

When I speak at Women in Business conferences, the same concerns come up from the audience: fear of failure, a confusion about which parts of themselves, if any, should be visible at work, persistent self-questioning, fear of judgement and a lot of impostor syndrome. These feelings are magnified in the wider workplace context, by issues such as the need to wait for the gender pay gap to be closed, or for diversity statistics to become more balanced.

Slightly controversial perhaps, but I don't want to engage in arguments about fairness – there are plenty of people fighting that battle. I truly believe that even when everything is fair, the difference between men and women will still be evident. As women we give ourselves a harder time than men, and we hold ourselves back more. This book is about opening your eyes to that and helping you see that this is not something you need to tolerate anymore.

I can help you to get to know yourself with these pages and see the brilliance that lies beneath the sea of self-doubt. You have to set the tone for all the other men and women who look up to you: the people in your organisation, your family members, even people who haven't been born yet. You can't wait any longer – you need to lead *now*. There are people following your lead right now, and if you play small, you are helping them stay small, too.

I worked myself into the ground because I thought my career was the most important thing in my life. In reality, I was using it as a mechanism to help me believe that I was good enough. What I wanted more than anything was someone to hand me my perfect future on a platter. I sacrificed relationships, my health and my personal growth to perform in each role, always reaching for the next big thing, but never understanding why. After many years of waiting for my success to happen and realising that I had given over control of my life to my bosses, I said, 'No more'. I looked at how I was spending my time, took a truthful deep dive into how little my efforts seemed to be paying off, and I got off the corporate ladder. Having trained as a coach in 2005, I finally set up my coaching business in 2014 and I haven't looked back. I didn't have self-awareness, courage or an understanding of my personal influence back then, but I do now. I am going to be your leader on this journey just like you will be to many others by the time you finish reading this book.

This book is designed to be read from beginning to end first time around – no dipping in and out until you have read it once through. After that, it may well become your reference book, the place you head to when you need clarity or a boost.

The book is laid out according to my tried and tested ABC model:

- **Part One – Awareness**

  I want you to start with part one, which is going to help you clarify who you really are and what it is you want to achieve in life. We will address all the areas where you are being limited and allowing your talents to be capped, and I will make the status quo look so unpalatable that you can't help but be hungry to take action.

- **Part Two – Bravery**

  In part two, I outline what it looks like to be a tiny bit braver than you are right now, so that we can generate evidence to show that you can and must take leadership now. It can't wait any longer. And the best bit – it isn't even scary! This part is about generating momentum, which is so much easier once part one is under your belt.

- **Part Three – Contribution**

  In part three, I am going to show you exactly how self-awareness and bravery, when performed consistently and repetitively, are going to make an unfathomable contribution to your own fulfilment as a leader, whether you think your current job is the one for you or not. This is about creating a new perspective for your personal and professional future *before* the circumstances show up. It is about how you make an impact with your personal leadership. All the time you fear you have wasted, and all the pigeonholes you believe you are in, they all count, and I will show you how to address these with tactics that have worked time after time with my clients.

At the end of each chapter, I am going to extract one thing that you can do to start making an impact on your life and your career in that moment:

 Part One – a question to ask yourself to unlock greater awareness

Part Two – an action requiring 1% more bravery to expand your comfort zone

 Part Three – an action that contributes to a bigger future

Make a commitment to yourself to act on those suggestions as a minimum. I promise they have the power to change your world and set the tone for the people looking to you for leadership.

This is going to be an exciting journey that will bring you relief. Never before has a path to career fulfilment been laid out so simply. It all starts with you – after all, you're the only factor in your career fully under your control. Show others how great they can be by being the best version of you.

PART ONE
AWARENESS

Did you read the introduction? I know, I rarely do either. But this one will clearly lay out the structure of this book and how to get the most from it. Go on… give it four minutes, it'll be worth it!

Part one of this book is about awareness: where you are now and what could be stopping you from reaching your end point. We are not seeking to solve issues with this part of the book; rather, I want to unlock your thinking and provide you with some explanation as to why you felt the need to pick up this book in the first place.

Let's get started.

Clarity

We spend a lot of time believing we don't know what we want. Maybe that's true, maybe it isn't. I'm going to clear the fog and help you see where you currently stand.

1. Confusion

Right now, you are confused. You have a great job, good friends and you even manage to have a social life. Yet somehow you feel flat. There are so many people who admire, even envy what you have, and here you are, unhappy with your lot. How can that be? Dare you even share these feelings with anyone?

It's OK. You are not alone.

Highly capable women like you often find themselves with an outer life to be admired and inner feelings that don't match. You have been getting promotions and consistently delivering, and you have been thinking that you were the one driving the bus of success. In fact, you have been allowing other people to decide where your capabilities are best housed. Flattered by someone thinking of you, you have been taking only the jobs offered to you.

Don't wait to be asked

'That's the problem with so many women in the workplace, we think careers are like a 1940s tea dance. Nice girls wait to be asked.'
— Anna Kessel

Every time someone expresses an opinion about your next role, or offers you one, you are so grateful that you entertain their vision. Maybe you believe it is a great job for you, so you go along with it. But do you stop to consider whether it is in line with what you want? Will it bring you the fulfilment you seek? If you don't consider your feelings at this point, in six months you will be back to thinking there is something wrong with you. What you are experiencing is a form of apathy. You're playing too small.

I may as well come clean and set the tone for this book now. I am going to be honest with you, and it might run close to the bone. It may be painful for you to confront your truths like this. But it's OK – I will never leave you without a solution.

The only thing wrong with you is this – you are looking to others to define what is 'good', and you are expending all your energy seeking approval that you are meeting their standards without a clear definition of what they are. The path you are on was laid by all the people who have gone before you. The trajectory is the one that is expected of you, and you have kept your head down and delivered against that plan. But it wasn't *your* plan. This is why you have been frustrated and sometimes resentful. Because the thing that you have been working so hard for might not actually be what you want.

If I asked you what you wanted now, would you be able to answer?

My guess is no. Because you have been so busy pleasing other people and not wanting to let people down that you haven't taken the time to ask yourself what you want. You'd think it was self-indulgent. Well, indulge away, because this book is all about you.

Wanting to please other people must somehow be in the DNA of all females. I can't think of a single woman I know who hasn't at some point chosen to put the needs, or perceived needs, of other people ahead of her own. We are prepared to go out of our way for others, yet we aren't willing to do the same for ourselves.

The thing about attempting to please other people before you please yourself is that deep down, you are looking for a pay-off. And when you attempt to fix other people without them asking for help first, you aren't going to get the recognition you are expecting, and hence what you need. Extrapolate this to all the relationships where you show up in this way, and you are at some point going to tip into feeling resentful. I'd like to save you the pain of that and refocus you now.

First lead yourself

You cannot lead other people until you have first led yourself.

You must start listening to what you need and go about giving it to yourself. In my 'Taking a Leap' online interview series recorded in 2016, Gabby Pelicci said something that rang so true: 'Your family are only as functional as you are.' This wasn't the first time I'd felt this as the mother of a small child. Putting your child's needs first is natural, but I would be no good to my daughter if I didn't look after my own well-being – my diet, my body and my mindset. This statement could be true for other aspects of your life – just substitute the word 'family': 'Your [*relationship, career, exercise habit*] is only as functional as you are.'

I am not talking about being self-absorbed here, but rather self-informed. Starting with you is essential. I realise that you won't be in the habit of doing this yet. This book will show you how in a number of different contexts. Play around with the content of this book. Create your own new evidence that disproves the beliefs that have been holding you back. Only when you start to put the focus on you will other people truly benefit.

We are going to work on the basis that you *are* good enough. I am not going to spend time convincing you of that. But I intend to show you what has been holding you back, and make you see how useless that has been, so you'll no longer want to settle in those patterns. Then I'll show you how you can leverage what you already have for better results, while having fun along the way. Sounds good, right?

It's as easy as ABC

Imagine a life where you have dreams, ones that excite you, and you have a plan that gets you from where you are today to that place, in a series of straightforward steps. This is possible when you:

1. Become *aware*

2. Take *brave* action

3. Make a *contribution*

This book is going to show you how to move from a place of confusion to one where you are consistently growing, enjoying the journey and are never at risk of hitting a plateau.

(?)

One question to ask yourself today:

What do you know for sure?

---

2. In-between energy

We have established that you don't really know what you want yet. That's probably better than me having to prise you away from what you think you want! I am guessing you aren't sitting there idle, wondering what to do with your time. I bet your life is actually moving pretty quickly, it's just not moving in the direction you want it to...

Whenever I meet a new client, the most impactful problem I can solve is what I call 'in-between energy'. You might know it as 'overwhelm' – where you have so many current commitments, habits and things to do, you cannot possibly consider anything new. Yet every time you go out to dinner with friends or are exposed to new people at conferences and networking events, you come home with another list of things you should be doing, but don't have space for. This further exacerbates the feeling of overwhelm. Obligation brings the heaviest weight.

A new idea may excite you for a while, but will fade without you having ever progressed it, leaving you with an emotional residue that is costly. It feeds your inner soundtrack of 'Well, there goes another idea you didn't action'.

When the noise has died down, you are left with the same life you had before you had the idea. Nothing changes, so you feel in limbo. Just sort of bobbing along between the life you have and the one you repeatedly dream of... and will eventually lament.

In-between energy plays out moment to moment, day to day. It is fuelled by all the lists you make and carry over to tomorrow, every time you say, 'I must remember to...' and you don't. When you do these things, you are parking decisions that feel too hard in the moment of overwhelm. Each time, you magnify in-between energy. That energy feels heavy, burdensome, repetitive and you want to shake it off. The only way to do that is to make decisions. If you don't, you are just in the car park, without hope of ever reaching a destination. It doesn't matter whether you are in the driving seat or not. The best you can hope for is survival. And each time you repeat this pattern you are, by default, choosing not to make any progress. It is debilitating. And guess what example that sets for those people following you? It throws them into confusion. They are looking at you and thinking: 'If someone is this capable, and they work this hard, how come they aren't getting the big job?' You are thinking it, and so is the next generation.

Are you marketing yourself in the best way here? Or are you teaching people that you are indecisive? Seemingly happy to stay in middle management, never reaching your true potential.

Paint a new picture – for you and them. Decide yea or nay, and clear the energy between one choice or another. Making decisions is something that feels loaded when you are in overwhelm, but the minute you make one, you'll feel relieved. It's about taking things off your plate, not adding more.

I'd like you to make a decision now. Decide that this is not going to be another self-help book you read and do nothing with. Decide that you are going to look honestly at yourself when I call you out. I am not going to read your mind perfectly, but if you feel yourself getting agitated, listen to that. Use it. It is something you should pay attention to, as it is the truth about your resistance being shown to you.

Space and clarity

I have used this process to help hundreds of clients gain clarity. It works like this:

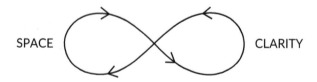

It is a cyclical process. The more space you create, the more clarity it brings. You become clearer about what will make an impact, and clearer about what to let go of, and so the cycle goes on. There is no end point.

My goal with this book is not to fix you, because you ain't broke! You are just experiencing in-between energy, which is making everything feel like hard work. When we clear it, the treacle you are wading through will dissolve, and you'll be able to focus on what you want.

So, have you decided? Are you with me?

Then clear your in-between energy now:

- If you are watching things on eBay, make a decision – buy them or unwatch them.

- Are there things in your online shopping basket? Buy them or delete them.

- Have you got something on your to-do list that keeps rolling over? Do it, ditch it or delegate it to someone else.

- Is there something pencilled in your diary that you haven't committed to? Ink it in or erase it.

- Have you got subscriptions for magazines you receive and never get around to reading? Cancel them.

- Are you paying for software you never use? Uninstall it.

- Have you got items you don't use that could benefit someone else? Give them away or list them for sale. Then put them out of sight until they are sold.

- Got ten different tabs open in your internet browser? Close them.

- Are you constantly distracted by app notifications? Turn them off, along with your data connection, when you are working on something important.

- Have you not responded to a friend's request to meet up? You either want to go or you don't. If you do, respect her and give her the dates. If not, tell her that realistically, it isn't going to happen in the next three months, and tell her why.

What I am effectively talking about here is decluttering – your physical and mental space alike.

Stop reading for a moment and think about three easy ways you can clear your in-between energy today. I urge you to go and do one of them now – at least one will involve your phone! Seriously, do one thing *now*. Begin your track record of being someone who takes actions that make a difference in real time. See the benefit of redeeming this energy straight away.

One question to ask yourself today:

**Where does your energy need
cleaning up the most?**

3. Where are you heading?

This question may have you with your head in your hands shouting, 'I don't know!' Let me relax you for a moment by saying that the answer doesn't have to be a fixed place that you must sign up with blood to reach. Quite the opposite. It is more a hypothetical place that we are seeking to prove is worthy of your talent, or not as the case may be.

When I thought I might want to become a teacher, I had the vision of Head of Media Studies in mind. I started to take my route towards that by shadowing in schools. But it became clear almost immediately that I would enjoy neither the journey nor the destination. I am asking about your direction, not pinning you down to a destination. Do you know what it is?

Many people start their careers and continue them with the goal of reaching the top. But not everyone wants to be the CEO or chairperson of the biggest company in the world. Or maybe some do, but they don't believe it will ever happen...

It is important before embarking on a journey to first define your direction. How many times have you set off in the car not knowing where you intend to go? Not often, I'd say. Yet when we start our careers, we often do so without having a clear end in mind. We aren't even actively exploring, we are just working hard, hoping someone notices, and that at some point you will be invited, expected or told to take the next rung on the ladder.

The right wall

> 'If the ladder is not leaning against the right wall,
> every step we take just gets us to the wrong place
> faster.'
> — Stephen R Covey

In my twenties, I didn't feel I had the experience or
knowledge of what was on offer to choose another
wall. At thirty, I trained as a coach: I knew the right
wall but didn't have the courage to prop the ladder
against it. At thirty-four, I started getting itchy feet.
Nothing was going quite as I had expected. I wasn't
married yet, I hadn't had two children, and, for
all the hard work I'd put in, I didn't want to admit
that my career wasn't living up to my hopes. While
I did change sector at this point from technology to
healthcare, this wasn't the move that reflected my true
desires. I was still being altruistic about why I wanted
what I wanted, as if pleasing myself would have me
cast out of society. Only when my fortieth birthday
was looming did I take action that made a real contribution towards becoming a full-time coach. It's amazing the urgency that a round-numbered birthday can
create!

The sad bit about this round-up of the last twenty
years is that it is the same pattern that nearly all of
my clients have gone through. Between thirty-four
and thirty-nine is the time when women really start
to question where their life is heading. At this age,
'I should be able to work this out on my own' often
keeps them where they are. Instead of investing in

themselves, they run away on holiday, only to return two weeks later even more miserable. And still lacking direction.

The longer it takes for you to focus on your own personal growth, the longer you put off the results. That's easy for me to say with hindsight! The sad outcome of remaining in self-reliance is the loss of five years on your life plan, during which you'll repeat all the habits and behaviours that got you there. As Marshall Goldsmith says, 'What got you here won't get you there.'

To generate change, you have to change something. Anything, frankly, just to break the pattern. Don't wait for another birthday, a health scare, or a professional slap in the face. I've had all of these, and the recovery from the emotions that follow just makes the journey harder. Now is the best time for you to put these things into action.

Maybe you've convinced yourself that life is OK. If so, you're settling for good enough. Good enough is flat. It won't excite you, it won't bring surprises and it definitely won't stand out enough to inspire other people. If you feel a sense of boredom right now, this is why. You are settling for good when you could be *great*.

This book is a pattern interruption.

Until now, you have been putting your ladder against a wall you can't see the top of, and are climbing like crazy. Let's apply this to another context to demonstrate how illogical it is – you decide to go on holiday, but you don't book anywhere, and you stand in the airport hoping someone will give you a ticket without you asking for it. Madness!

So, before you go any further in life or your career, let's take the time to define where you are heading. Do you want the top job? What is it about the top job that is attractive to you? What is it that repels you? There is clarity to be had in answering both of these questions.

Don't settle for second place

I remember when my mum had a tarot card reading when I was still at school. She came back happy to announce that I was going to be a hugely competent wing-woman someday. A reputable second in command. This excited me – it sounded like I'd be the person who was best-performing but who didn't have the pressure of being at the top. In my early teens I knew this, despite never having entered a workplace. I am guessing it was a reflection of my mother's desire to play safe, work hard and never, ever stick one's head above the parapet.

Remind you of anyone? Nearly every female client I have ever had has wanted that position of second in command. Let me spell out why:

1. She wants the world to depend on her. She wants to be core to everyone else's success because it

gives her purpose. But she also wants the kudos (even though when she gets it, she bats is straight back – more on this in the chapter about impostor syndrome).

2. She believes that the top job comes with pressure, undesirable visibility and, above all, sacrifices.

The reality is that the top job is arguably easier than the second in command. The second in command is running the show while the top job manages relationships: with shareholders, board members, partners, the marketplace. The second in command is more operational. She is the one who is going to be the escalation point for issues. It's therefore more unpredictable a role in terms of its demands on time needed to be dedicated to the job.

When you are a person who leaves decisions about your future to the person above you, you are making the ultimate sacrifice. It doesn't get any worse than that. Take back the power by defining the top and the route you'll follow to get there. It's freeing. It doesn't add pressure, it diffuses it.

The top job is one where there are commitments, but you have a certain freedom to define strategy – what the leadership team looks like, its ethos, its values. Judging whether or not you want to be in the top job cannot be based on who has gone before you. Getting that job is about setting your own agenda and painting a vision that people can get excited by, buy into and actively contribute towards. Before you get up there, you'll not only have to define where 'there' is, but you'll need to take the reins of your career and become the authority on its design.

Now is the time to check that your ladder is against the right wall. There is no point climbing it relentlessly if it's leading you to a place of emptiness, confusion and unfulfilment. I am going to help you to become more aware of who you are, what you really want – when you aren't pleasing other people – and what value only *you* can bring to an organisation. Get ready, because that organisation may one day be your own.

Your top might not be *the* top. We are conditioned to think we should all want to be CEO. For me, the top needed to be a place where I could have influence. I realised when I got to my top that I only got there *because* of my influence. In other words, I'd had influence all along.

Defining the top is about setting your direction – it's a place you can head towards. Without direction, you won't move. You won't make progress. At every step, you should ask yourself whether the direction you are heading in still feels good.

Before heading further, let's check your motivations.

One question to ask yourself today:

What do you want to see in the workplace?

4. Check your motivations

Now is an appropriate time to ask… Why do you even want a promotion?

Can you actually answer that? I remember when my first coach asked me why I wanted to be Director of Marketing – I was stumped. Reasons like, 'Doesn't everyone in marketing want to be the director?' were going around my head. What am I doing in my current role (Head of Product Development) if it's not to be in position to take the next rung on the ladder?

Seriously. Stumped.

When I was asked to take up the Acting Director position, I thought I had it made. I felt important, recognised and rewarded – only by title, as the money hadn't yet followed. I was a rock star at work and frankly, this step up had been a long time coming. Yet still I wasn't able to answer the question – why do I want to be in that job?

I know now that all the reasons I wanted to reach that heralded position were related to my ego. My 'status anxiety', as Alain de Botton would call it, was rife. I wanted the title, the money, the control. I wanted a permanent seat around the right tables, not to be there merely as a guest presenter. As I looked long and hard at my motivations, I just wanted the attention. It would reward all the effort I had put in to get there.

But when I got there, I felt none of these things. I felt empty. Why? Because none of it was meaningful. I had been a leader all along. I'd been doing it naturally. I thought that something would change once I had the title as well. It didn't. It just served to confuse me and led me to ask myself: Why am I doing this? Why did I want this so much? And if I'm here already, what now?

I didn't want my boss's job. All of a sudden, at the age of twenty-eight, I didn't know what the future looked like. I had been racing up a ladder that was against the only wall I'd had in my vision. My coach helped me see that there was a whole load of other walls. I didn't see that as an opportunity then – it terrified me.

The problem with committing years to one particular career is that you become blinded to all the others that exist. With each additional year you dedicate to your sole endeavour, it feels like another nail in your coffin. If you can relate, you are definitely reading the right book!

What I realised is that my ego had me focused on all the wrong things. From my viewpoint, everything seemed limited. The only options before me were ones that other people had already explored, jobs that already existed and were occupied by people who had no plans to go anywhere else. My career growth seemed impossible, stunted, and I needed to break free.

I made a bold move and went to be a director somewhere else for a lot more money. Finally, I had broken the six-figure salary mark, under the age of thirty. Maybe this is what the gap was? No. Three months in, I realised that money had not taken away the vacuous nature of my working life. I was capable but bored, underchallenged and losing my sense of self as each day ticked on.

What was lacking was the possibility that I could make meaningful impact. I didn't really care about making bigger profits or selling more widgets. One day all of it would be replaced by new technology, but I would be using the same product development process and asking the same board members to approve my new business cases. My life was predictable, and I didn't like it one bit.

I wanted to play bigger. I wanted my work to bring real significance to people and the world I'd one day raise kids in. I began my search for purpose.

Purposeful impact

The McKinsey report on 'Achieving World Class Productivity in the NHS' had just gone public and it hinged on bringing market management skills into the sector. It was like a light bulb went on and I thought, 'Yes! I have those and I can make an important difference to the economy and the wellbeing of the country.' Absolutely everyone I spoke to in my network advised me against it, but I didn't listen. 'It's too institutionalised,' they said. 'Even you can't make a difference in the NHS.'

I believed I could make a difference, but I am sad to say, several years on, that this lone, corporate rock star didn't change the system. Yes, customer service in Outpatients got better because of my transformation projects, but actually, it was the lives I changed through my style and conversations that made the real difference. I realised that the way I challenged people's thinking was somewhat unique.

This is the part that had been missing all along. Purposeful impact – on people, not processes or products. On the way that people showed up and the impact they would have on the other people they communicated with.

Building connection is what will change the world. It is how the world will become a better place. Businesses can focus on what they are good at when they have at the helm incredible employees doing jobs that reflect their passion.

So, are you motivated by ego or impact?

If you have just realised that you have been spending all your time giving in the hope of receiving, allowing your qualities to be magnified just because you have a certain title or, worse, holding back because you don't yet have the title you want, then you are led by ego. Let me get this out of the way now.

Money and a title will not give you what you need. Leadership is never given; it is available to you any time you choose to take it. And people are waiting to follow.

I will spend the rest of this book advising you how to clear your path so you can remove the obstacles that *you* are putting in your way, so you can stop waiting for permission and start leading. This doesn't mean that you'll be stepping on people's toes. It means that you will bring clarity and vision to other people, such that they choose to be inspired by and subsequently align themselves to your way of being and doing.

For me, the missing piece I had been looking for all along was about the difference I wanted to make. If your goals are stopping short, we need to make them bigger. We'll cover this next.

One question to ask yourself today:

Who are you prepared to be in the workplace?

5. Think bigger

I am going to assume that you have been motivated by ego to date… if you're honest, that is. There is no point being any other way on this personal growth journey.

Being the best you can possibly be just for you, how-ever, tells me that you are playing small. Dare I say, even, that you are being selfish. You are capable of so much more than you think and stopping out your goals before you have truly made a difference in the world is a crying shame.

When you've come from confusion and in-between energy, it is easy to think that all you want is for things to be calm and clear. Focusing on your career ambition or your balance between work and family time feels impossible. But calm is just an interim goal, a new baseline. Once there, it's time to think bigger. Trust that this book will give you that perspective. Let me ask you, then…

What are your career ambitions for?

The 'Which means that…' technique

Now is the time to dream. A colleague taught me the 'Which means that…' technique. Earl was in sales and I was in marketing. It was my first product manage-ment job, and his advice helped me bring to life the features and benefits of my services that sat flat on a page until that point. You want to lead the Women's Council or be the Director of Strategy, great. Why? What difference are you going to make when you are in that role?

Your goals can't stop at getting the job. I had a goal to write this book, but writing it isn't enough. I could achieve that and leave it safely hidden on my USB drive for the rest of my life. Or I could use it to make a difference in the world.

Here's an example of how I enlarged my thinking with the 'Which means that…' technique:

I want to write a book, which means that I need to get it published, which means that you can buy it, which means that you will read it, which means that you can stop wasting time and energy on the stuff that doesn't make a difference, which means that you can move up the ladder in your career in a more powerful and efficient manner, which means that you can spend more quality time with your friends and family, which means that you will be happier and have greater energy, which means that you have more in the tank to inspire, which means that you will generate more self-confidence, which means that you will voice your vision on bigger platforms, which means that more people will hear the message that I have helped you get clear on, which means that you will lead people to a better way of living, which means that you can reach more people in the world, which means that people will be happier in their working lives, which means that people in general will be more fulfilled with their existence on the planet.

Do you see?

I can't just write a book – that isn't enough. And you can't just get a promotion.

What do you want to change? Make a difference to? What's this all for?

Your goals aren't all about you. There are people in the world whose lives you, and only you, can make better. They need you to reveal the leader within to make the difference they don't know they can yet. They are counting on you. Are you up for it?

You have to be the leader *they* want to see.

Ask yourself what you are enabling with every single thing you want and do. If you are not bringing about positive change, then the thing you are doing has no real value. This should bring you huge relief. You may of course then choose to focus on all the time you have wasted to date, but guess what, that would be a further waste of your time! Instead, imagine if you could clear the decks completely in order to focus on thinking bigger. What would you have on the agenda? Would you put back everything that is currently on there? I think not. You would *only* bring back the stuff that counts.

That is what this book is about. Getting you clear on where you are now, and getting you clear on what has been stopping you, so we can move those things to one side. Then you'll be able to see your bigger vision and begin your path towards it. Simple! By the time you have finished this book, that is exactly what you will be thinking.

Use your head wisely

There is a school of thought called mBraining (multiple braining). It works on the basis that we all possess at least three brains – not just the cephalic brain in the head, but the cardiac brain in the heart and the enteric brain in the gut. They all contain neurons and have the power to make decisions. Deep down, you know this. You hear of them when people say, 'Think about it.' Or, 'My heart isn't in it.' Or, 'I need to digest this.'

It's a global statement, but one that I think will ring true: women overthink things. And the outcome of those thoughts rarely goes in our favour. My main role in coaching is to get people out of their heads. When you are motivated by impact, your three brains are in balance. When you stop the analysis and the running of worst-case scenarios in your head, you can allow your heart brain to take over and dream about what you'd love to do, be, or have. If a knot forms in your stomach, you'll know that this contradicts who you really are, for this is where your true identity lies.

You may tell yourself you'd love to teach, for example, but if the thought of standing in front of a room of teenagers turns your stomach, then your gut instinct is trying to tell you something. It isn't a match for you. When you prioritise your vision for the future based on your heart and gut, you can use your head for its main purpose – creative thinking, planning, problem-solving and genuine risk assessment.

When in doubt, tune into your heart brain, show yourself some compassion and ask if your heart is in this, and what impact you want to make.

You now know that the journey isn't as hard as it first appeared. That is purely the perspective of the lens you have been looking through to date. Your overused head didn't really understand why you were working so hard, because it had no direction against which it could measure your progress. I know you know you are capable, but I also know that you don't trust yourself to make the right decision. Rest assured, this is simply a characteristic of spending too much time in your head, of choosing confusion. There is nothing wrong with you, you just haven't unlocked the goldmine of talent that lies within you yet.

None of what I am going to ask you to do requires you to learn more or do more. It requires you to trust and believe in yourself so you stop trying so hard to fit irrelevant moulds. These are both characteristics of your gut.

The job you want, the one that is destined to house your talents, probably doesn't exist yet, so you don't need to fit anyone's mould. You need to be more of who you already are. It is this purest version of you that will inspire others to be themselves and get you one step closer to a world without pretence. When you allow the space for your head to be creative, the path will soon emerge.

Let's look at some of the patterns keeping you stuck.

One question to ask yourself today:

**What's the ultimate impact you
would love to make?**

Why You're Stuck

Now we know where you are, let's work out the patterns that got you there, and shake them up a bit. Keep in mind that patterns are not something we fall into. They are something we choose when we have nothing better to focus on.

6. Are you a busy fool?

Deep down, we all know that being busy is not a measure of success, yet we step into the trap of thinking that we're being productive. We believe if we are busy, then we have purpose, but it simply isn't true.

We judge people that seem to be able to take downtime. Sitting on the sofa with a cuppa and a magazine is just plain lazy, isn't it? Not really, no. 'Busy' is not a badge of honour.

I was on the London underground recently and I witnessed a conversation that demonstrates this perfectly.

> HER: Hey, long time no see.
> HIM: Yeah (*long sigh*).
> HER: How are things?
> HIM: Oh, you know. Busy.
> HER: What have you been up to?
> HIM: Well, you know, just keeping busy. Work, the kids... It's just so busy.

You may notice the lack of detail. This man has staked his claim on busy, like most people who feel overwhelmed do, and is so resigned to being that way that he can't tell you specifically what he has been doing. If you asked him if he was making progress, you would probably blow his mind! All he achieved with this conversation is the possibility that the next time this woman sees him on the train, she might bury her head in her copy of *Metro*.

I get it. When I was in a corporate job, I used to pride myself on having to run to the loo as quickly as possible, would bring sandwiches into meetings and ask my PA to bring my coffee. When I sat at my desk, I would have a queue of people waiting to talk to me. While that annoyed me sometimes, my ego loved it. The need to be needed trumped my annoyance every time. I was the cog at the centre of all the wheels and I loved it. Until I didn't anymore...

What changed? I realised in a spectacular penny-dropping moment that running myself ragged wasn't actually getting me anywhere. This habit was costing me professionally, on top of taking an obvious mental and physical strain. I have no doubt that being in the busy trap is costing you in the same ways.

While I was making myself indispensable over here, people over there were saying I was too valuable to be moved up the ladder: 'Look how busy she is, we can't possibly let her move into another department – everything would fall apart without her.' Making yourself critical to the box you are currently ticking will indeed probably bring you the security you sought when you started that behaviour, but it will also keep you boxed in. It will keep you stuck. Being busy is the best way to remain stationary.

My schedule also had absolutely no room in it. Sound familiar? Are you in back-to-back meetings, without time for lunch? Are you rushing out the door to collect children or trying not to be late to dinner with friends? A good day to you might look like one where you get to places on time. But what about the impact you make when you get there? Do you actually enjoy the food? Do you engage with your friend? Do you listen to your child, or are you looking at your phone for the next distraction?

What if something urgent were to happen? What then? The reality is that you would have to drop one of your current commitments. The question is, why should you need to wait for a disaster before you will reprioritise your day?

When I first shifted to not giving all the answers, not being available for every meeting requested and sending a deputy instead, it felt like self-exclusion. But it quickly became clear that I had freed myself up to contribute to the future I wanted, to create and attend the meetings that would truly move the needle, would make a real difference.

I didn't need to make my *now* bigger, I needed to clear the path to my bigger future.

Mic drop…

The reason you felt the need to be so busy in the first place was to prove your worth to other people, to feel important and useful, but this isn't what we commonly know as purpose these days. You can't get to a bigger vision if you are trying to prove your worth in the current circumstances. You're already in those, so you don't need to prove anything!

More importantly, you are expending an awful lot of energy, like the man on the underground, doing things you can't even describe. I know you are highly capable, and you pride yourself on delivery, so focus on impact. Get clear on what you want to be, feel, and do – that may look a lot like slowing down rather than cramming more in.

In order to get clarity, you have to make space. The more space you make, the more clarity you'll get.

EXERCISE: DRAINS AND RADIATORS

Drains steal your energy; radiators give out more. What saps your energy? Going to the supermarket, phoning utility companies, or seeing that friend that only talks about herself? Let some of these things go and you will not only clear time, but you will see your energy reappear. I realise you have probably just had an inner meltdown... partly because you know this already and haven't addressed it, but also because you don't know how to communicate to someone that you don't want to see them, or to ask for help. We are going to cover how to clearly communicate empathetically, don't worry. For now, I want you to have an awareness of your energy. Where is it being drained from you?

After you plug your drains, your radiators can start working. Who are the people who bring you warmth and lift you up? What are the tasks that you can lose hours doing because you just get in the zone? Where are the places that you come alive? In a forest, by a lake? Once a month, I move my workplace for the day to a café in a nature reserve or I run my retreat in the forest. It not only replenishes me, but it is normally my most productive time.

Start becoming aware of what makes you tick. Your energy is something you sense. There is a big difference between a sigh because you're exhausted and a sigh when you reach the peak of a long walk and take in the view, or when you sit down and drink a cup of coffee while it is still hot, or read a page of a magazine without anyone interrupting you. These things don't happen by accident, they are done intentionally. First you have to know you want them and value the impact they'll have on your energy.

Remember, being busy is not only a waste of focus, but it is also blooming tiring! Focus on the tasks that make the difference, the people that light you up and the spaces that bring you joy. It took me a long time to realise that I am not an extrovert. My energy comes largely from within. Once I got comfortable with who I am, I started to like my own company, and I didn't need everyone else's approval anymore. This started with me slowing down and creating some space between tasks to check that I was actually enjoying them. Start getting to know yourself today. You might even like what you see…

One question to ask yourself today:

What if you had no to-do list?

7. Hell is other people

I am going to tell you what I tell all of my clients when we start working together, which is, I am not coaching anyone else. I am *your* coach, so let's not waste precious time focused on other people. Let's not get bogged down in stories or assumptions about them, and what that means for you. Half the time, what you are worried about is what you think other people are thinking, not what they actually think or said.

My first coach gave me some sage advice: either assume the best or ask. Given that most people don't have the courage to ask, it is more straightforward to do the former, and have a healthy disregard for our beliefs about things that have not been said and that we don't know for sure. When you are about to give a presentation at work, assume that the people in the room believe your content is going to impact them positively. Believe that you are pretty special to be the one standing at the front of the room doing something most other people wouldn't do. And by doing it, you are inspiring other people to believe that perhaps they can do it too.

I don't focus on things that don't help me. I especially don't focus on what negativity people might be projecting onto me, and I urge you not to either. When we receive negative feedback, or we sense that something is aimed at us, we need to be impartial. Identify where the comment came from. An example would be if someone says, 'It's alright for you…' then I know that what they are about to say is about them.

That person feels jealous of something I appear able to do or have that they believe they can't. That's not something I need to take on. Equally, if someone says my content offended them, I will consider whether or not it was offensive or whether the other person was being particularly sensitive. I would trust my gut on this.

We can't know for sure what goes on in other people's heads, so we can either ask to clear the in-between energy, or we can practise assuming the best. The latter is easier and preferable – it means you don't need to go to the effort of setting up a time to talk, and it also gives you control over how you respond to your environment.

When I am speaking on stage and I look out at my audience, I don't always get laughter and smiles. Sometimes I get serious faces and what looks like boredom. I have collected evidence over the years to prove that these are often 'thinking faces', or people who are zoning in to what I am saying, not zoning out. I choose to believe this is true of everyone in my audience. The people that this isn't true for don't impact me – they will never speak to me or engage with me if what I said didn't resonate with them.

Focus on you while you read this book. This is your journey. Be selfish about it. You'll realise that 'selfish' isn't such a dirty word as the book goes on.

Stop comparing

> 'Comparison is the thief of joy.'
> — Theodore Roosevelt

Looking at others and comparing yourself is rarely helpful. Some people believe that competition is healthy, and firmly believe that it eggs them on to do better, but the motivation behind this belief is actually the ego. Why is it that you need to be better than someone else? Is that person someone you hold in high esteem, or are they the enemy that you want to take down?

Think about when you are on LinkedIn, and you see someone has a new job. How many times are you really happy for them, and how many times are you even a little jealous or bitter about the news? You start thinking, 'But they aren't even that good, and they aren't even that nice!' Perhaps not, but they have done something that has got your attention.

They got out of their seat in the audience and joined in the game. They have actively accepted the risk of potential rejection by putting themselves forward for a job, and they happen to have got it. And in the meantime, there you are, still in your seat, passing comment. Staying in your seat or not speaking up in meetings is a downward spiral. That feeling of disappointment you have in yourself will only grow until you stop it. So, *stop it!*

Comparing yourself to other people is negative. What's worse, when you compare yourself to others and attempt to copy them, you just look like another version of that person. No one will remember you. Do you now realise that this is what you have been doing to date? No wonder they have the job and you don't. Sorry to be blunt, but that is what will continue to happen until you leave your seat.

A helpful form of comparison looks at your own behaviour – nobody else's. Start by assessing how you perform now compared with the last time you did the same activity. Perhaps that is public speaking, writing an important email, dealing with a conflict with a project team member – whatever the activity is that you believe is going to count towards being a more confident version of yourself. Strive to be better and define that any way you like.

For me, I strive to be better in so many ways that are not aligned with the person I used to show up as at work. I used to say I wanted to be better, faster, more x, y and z. All of those things were coming from a place of I am not x, y or z enough.

Now my life and the roles I play are more closely related to my values, so I strive to be kinder, a better listener, more vulnerable, more honest. These are things I am already, but I know that there is room for growth. I have the potential to be a better coach, speaker, friend, partner, child and mother. None of these things are benchmarked against anyone else, only myself.

When I was a young director in the City of London, my intended end point was a place where I would be accepted by others and defined as good enough to get the big job. Now my end point is the best version of me. I don't know what that looks like, but I am curious to find out, and I measure my progress based on how the journey feels. That end point is not a place anyone else can reach. It is unique to me, so there is no competition. I can take my time.

In a 2019 press conference, Formula One star Lewis Hamilton said, 'There is no end to reach.' He described himself as 'working on a masterpiece and (he hasn't) quite finished yet'. At the time, he was five-time world champion, and has gained another title since. I am sure that statistic will also be out of date soon – that's his intention and where his efforts and energy are focused. He's not wasting time comparing himself to other drivers or other people's world records. He is systematically paying attention to being better than he was yesterday. That's it.

The process of reaching my end point or yours is not one of looking at others, it is one of looking within and measuring your success based on whether or not you feel better. My success is measured by the number of great conversations I have that reach way deeper than the surface level where my ego operates. From those conversations come friendships, and people being vulnerable about what they need, often generating more requests to coach, speak and support people.

There is no business plan or strategy involved here. By being more myself and disregarding what other people's paths look like, I am getting closer to being the purest, most truthful version of myself. The best words to describe this destination are 'at peace'.

This is ultimately what we all want – to feel enough. To silence our inner critic and be happy with the contribution we are making. This allows us to deeply connect with others and really make a difference.

You might not have the title of leader yet. You might not feel like you are in charge of anything, but believe me, you are. You are in charge of your own life. You are demonstrating leadership somewhere, such that others are following you. Those people, who could be friends or colleagues, are looking at you to influence them. Don't sell them a story that it is safer to stay in your seat. Show them that it is OK to get up and look around at what might be available, to participate in games they may not have played before, with you or anyone else. Show them that it is OK to make mistakes about what you really want on the way to clarity. Let them see who you are, so they can be who they are. Be part of the movement that unlocks other people, starting with letting me help you do the same.

---(?)---

One question to ask yourself today:

Who would you love to connect with?

---

8. Impostor syndrome

In case you have been hiding in a cupboard for most of your life and haven't heard about this phenomenon, impostor syndrome is where an individual repeatedly doubts their accomplishments and has a persistent fear of being found out.

If you haven't heard of it, this is *not* the moment you should go and look it up. It is not desirable and I will give you a much better alternative in this chapter. My intention is that those words never exit your mouth again!

Impostor syndrome is, typically, not something that people who haven't accomplished anything feel. It is something that people with a catalogue of successes experience often in their career. They don't seem to be able to hear all the praise and congratulatory remarks. It doesn't matter that the board presentation they just gave got approved or the programme of work that just got delivered reinforced their rock star status, or that they are getting testimonials from internal and external customers. They still feel like the situation is only temporary, that someone will call their name and say, 'Your luck has run out.'

The constant fear of being fired is something I can relate to. I got fired from my first two jobs. (You won't see that on LinkedIn!) The fear of being fired means that you are constantly trying to prove your worth. Making yourself seem more valuable than other people looks like working longer hours (the busy trap), covering up for people who under-deliver so the project you're on doesn't fail, becoming the hub for everything so you make yourself critical to all successes. I can relate – I was that person. The problem was, it came at a cost to me. It is costing you, too.

Supposedly women suffer from impostor syndrome more than men. Here's what I think is really going on. Everyone feels this way. Everyone who is advancing in their career and sticking their head above the parapet feels like the rug might be pulled from underneath them at any given moment, because there is a degree of risk about moving forwards. But what is the alternative? Stay still and bored for the rest of your life, wondering what might have happened if you had displayed a tiny bit of courage?

That isn't a viable option and you know it, which is why you are reading this book. The difference between men and women is that women often look for a label that they can associate with and hang their coat on. Men tend not to need those so much. They may feel exactly the same, they just don't seem to talk about it as much as women do. Women like to bond over their inadequacy – we are tribal that way. We want to know that someone else feels like us, so we are not alone. Knowing you are not alone might bring you relief, but it doesn't move you forward.

The Unicorn Effect

Owning impostor syndrome might bring a moment of clarity about what you are feeling, but it doesn't help you to do anything with it. We could choose any label, so why choose this one? In a talk I gave in 2019, I offered up an alternative, the Unicorn Effect. I define it as:

A psychological pattern in which a person assumes the best, and trusts that if they are true to themselves, they are capable of anything they focus on and they deserve it, too.

When I asked if anyone had heard of it, someone had, even though my eight-year-old and I had made it up the night before. That's how keen we are to look for labels! When I asked which one looked more helpful, impostor syndrome or the Unicorn Effect, the audience agreed unanimously that the Unicorn Effect would benefit them more.

You can't benefit from a syndrome – it is going to label you as stuck and give you reasons to stay stuck. It will have you constantly searching for proof of its existence and will become the reason you don't do what you desire. An effect, however, can be something that propels you forwards positively, and helps you achieve what you set out to.

So, if you insist upon choosing a label, why not choose the Unicorn Effect?

Break the pattern you have been choosing until now. You can *choose* to believe whatever you want. Why not this? Assuming the best means that you can take what looks like a painful situation, like actually being fired, and reframe it to make it count. When I was fired the first time, I believed, 'I have just dodged a bullet. This business was clearly not a good fit for me, and now I am on the fast track to something bigger and better.' Sure enough, I was. When I look back, none of what I have now would have happened if I hadn't been fired. I thought I was in my dream industry. How wrong I was.

Reframing helps you see that things that have already happened *had* to happen that way for you to make the decision in front of you right now. Make that decision count, and pick a perspective that is helpful. Choose to be positive and forward-focused instead of staying in pain.

If you can learn to take the negativity out of every situation, it can help you to be better. Impostor syndrome is probably putting you in a permanent state of stress and panic, worrying that someone is going to question your work or give you feedback that you have done something wrong. If you were benefitting from the Unicorn Effect, you would look for why this *had* to happen, and think, 'Thank goodness I got this feedback now – I might have wasted time going in the wrong direction. Now I can focus on what's most impactful.' In the long run, this approach will massively improve your confidence. And it will have you banking positive evidence that you can rely on later.

Reframing is a powerful tool. It is key to contribution – the art of making everything count.

Next time you catch yourself looking through the lens of an impostor, take just one aspect of the Unicorn Effect, apply it and ask yourself which is easier. Impostor syndrome will never win that battle, so let's dump it right now, shall we?

One question to ask yourself today:

What is the first thing you see through Unicorn Effect lenses?

9. No one is looking at you

Everyone I know experiences a fear of judgement in some capacity or another. I used to be crippled by it, and it exacerbated all my feelings of being an impostor.

Judgement has largely negative connotations. When you Google it, you see images of fire burning, pictures of begging God for forgiveness, courtroom gavels, etc. The memory that always crosses my mind is when I tried online dating and felt like I was literally losing and gaining points every time I uttered a sound!

In real life, it feels pretty scary to be judged. We get momentarily excited when we are nominated for something or shortlisted, only to have that feeling quashed a moment later when we consider how we might communicate the possible rejection if we don't win, and what our peers might think of that. The fear of judgement makes us lose all perspective.

Our inner critic doesn't think we should get ahead of ourselves. We think we might like that job, and then we read the spec looking for confirmation that we aren't good enough. Deciding not to bother trying before someone else can have the chance to judge us is a form of self-protection.

Judgement is rarely delivered carefully or sensitively. Not a lot of thought is put into how it will land, and it often hurts. So when we have an idea that opens us up to this risky feeling, we ping back to safety and decide that perhaps it is better to just stay as we are.

Once again, we are tempted to settle for the car park where there is no immediate danger, rather than the road that might take us somewhere. But you won't progress that way, therefore you won't be fulfilled.

The first step towards shifting this feeling is to connect with how pointless it is to fear judgement. Regardless of your fear, you are going to be left feeling unfulfilled. You may well give up because you deem the result unlikely to go your way. Are you prepared to sign up to a lifetime of staying where you are?

I genuinely believe it is challenging to stay in that place where you are a passenger in life and everyone else is in the driving seat. At some point, you will get fed up of that feeling. And you will start to show your resentment.

You could decide to play safe. You don't offend anyone, because you don't speak up. You bite your tongue in a bid to please others. You work hard and just hope that at some point, someone notices. Sometimes people do notice, but being this passive is rarely rewarded. This won't bring you fulfilment, either. And it definitely doesn't have you making an impact.

Eventually you'll get so fed up with yourself and others that you start speaking up, but it comes out all wrong because you are feeling resentful by this point. What you are communicating sounds like complaining and blaming, and then people start to call you aggressive. I get it. I have been there, too.

There is nothing valuable about staying in fear of judgement. It completely taints all of your communication. Yes, it's possible to move forward in spite of it, but you are making much harder work for yourself.

This book is about getting you to the top of your game while being a fantastic leader on the journey. Carrying a weight of fear of judgement with you will just get in your way. The only way to lead with ease and true grace is to get rid of it. Here's how...

Stop judging other people

> 'When you judge another, you don't define them, you define yourself.'
> — Wayne Dyer

What we give out, we get back. Our fear of judgement is a mirror of our own behaviour. If we fear judgement, it must be because we are judging.

When you go to a restaurant and you're a vegetarian, you won't even look at the meat menu. Why would you? People who don't judge other people don't consider for a moment that they will be judged. It isn't on their radar.

Let's work out where you are judging other people, in the spirit of fun. I want you to be giggling to yourself at this point, not judging how judgy you are! Do you get annoyed when you give way to someone in the car and they don't thank you? Do you pass comment on the behaviour of other people's children? Do you judge an outfit or hairdo, or someone at work who isn't being kind enough? Do you think they are being unprofessional or not delivering 'properly'?

Take a minute to list the areas where you judge others. It doesn't matter if this is a long list (it may well be), this chapter is about making you aware of where you are judging others. My list was *long* at the beginning of my journey. The good news is, the longer the list, the easier it will be to make a difference to your level of fear.

Over the course of the next week, you might see that you judge *a lot*. Here is your opportunity. Pick one area on your list where you can make a change easily. Driving without commentary is a major achievement for me. I recommit to it every single time I get in the car. Be kind to yourself when you make your recommitment and accept that it might be required every time you are around other people, initially.

When we judge others, we make it OK to be judged by others. If we judge or belittle *ourselves*, we also make it OK to be judged by others. Judging others is, in effect, *inviting* judgement upon ourselves.

As you stop judging, you will feel your fear lifting. You will start noticing that your acceptance muscle starts being flexed in its place, and you will stop seeing and hearing judgement where it perhaps never even existed. By stopping our judgement of others, we can release ourselves from the fear that keeps us playing small.

REAL-LIFE EXAMPLE: NO ONE IS LOOKING AT YOU

One of my training clients back in 2005 used to attend dance classes at Danceworks in central London. She lost out on joy because of her fear of judgement. At the end of the class, half of the dancers would perform that day's routine first, followed by the other half. One day I went with her and noticed that all of the people in the resting half were looking anxious – they were worried about their own performance. None of them were watching the first half's performance. They didn't care about the other people. They were too worried about themselves. They were so in fear of their own judgement that they didn't have time to judge their classmates' dancing. When I looked over at the first half, every single dancer was looking at themselves in the mirror. Not one of the thirty young women in that dance studio was judging anyone else. They were each too preoccupied with themselves.

When you stop judging everyone else, you'll realise no one is looking at you.

Let others see you for the reasons you decide upon. Set an example of never speaking about other people unless it is praiseworthy. Soon, people will follow your lead without even realising.

---⊘---

One question to ask yourself today:

What would you do if no one was watching and couldn't pass judgement?

---

10. Expectations

As babies, very little is expected of us. We eat, sleep, poop, and that's about it. All our parents want from us really is a facial expression that they can loosely associate with a smile every now and again. The bar is low. Then we go to school and suddenly, there are rules. We must be somewhere on time, behave in a certain way, and ask permission before we leave the room. And this sets the tone for life, doesn't it? Before we know it, we are being graded for work, interviewed for jobs and putting ourselves out there to have or not have relationships. This is why all the fears we have discussed in this first part of the book arise.

Expectations are set up based on history. By default, we assume things will happen as they always have for us, in the same way that they did for the people that went before us. It's as if the arena has already been set and our only job is to play our game within it. Stifling, right?

We see superstars, athletes and CEOs as the minority, often exceptions to the rules, but they are just people who had a bigger vision for themselves and decided to live up to it. Their expectations were that they would go beyond the achievements of their parents, friends or colleagues. Raising your expectations, therefore, is the first step to creating a bigger game and playing at the top of it.

The power of 'yet'

> 'If you think you are beaten, you are
> If you think you dare not, you don't,
> If you like to win, but you think you can't
> It is almost certain you won't.'
> — Walter D Wintle

Our thoughts bring about our reality. You may know that intellectually, but if you were living by it, honestly, you probably wouldn't be reading this book right now. It is likely you have introduced 'yes, but' into your consciousness, preventing you from living it practically.

Professional athletes have no guarantee that they will excel, and even when they do, they might not make the final cut, but they are committed to trying. When you say you can't do something, can you honestly say that you've given it your best try? Compare 'I can't' with 'I've never tried, but maybe I can.' Or, 'I'm rubbish at chess' versus 'I haven't won a game of chess *yet.*' One has a forgone conclusion wrapped up in it, the other is open to the possibility that it might just happen. Use 'yet' to introduce some grey into your black and white world.

When you have low expectations, you typically reject positive feedback because it is not in line with what you expect or think you deserve. If so, you are teaching people that you aren't to be valued. You probably don't even realise you're doing it. Those people will follow your lead. When your name crops up in conversation as a potential candidate for a promotion, they will discount you, just like you discounted yourself. Stop!

Rejecting positive comments comes from a place of low expectations. Low expectations stop you hearing and seeing what is positive – all the evidence that tells you your vision needs to expand. Think about it now, what do people tell you all the time that you reject? What would happen if you started listening to what people are *actually* saying? All the great feedback that you refuse to own will either keep coming until you listen, or it will dry up, because you have taught people that it is unwelcome. In fact, to you, the receiver, it currently makes no difference which of these it is, because your refuse to take it on.

Where are your expectations?

EXERCISE: WHAT WOULD YOU WISH FOR?

If I could just wave a magic wand, what would you have me do for your life? Change something in the workplace, adapt you as a parent or partner – what would it be? Maybe you'd ask to lose weight, maybe you just want the family to put their washing in the basket? It doesn't have to be a big wish, just something I could immediately change for you. Spend thirty seconds considering what that might be.

Now have a look at whether you were trying to get away from something or move towards it. This tells me something about your level of expectation of your future, and how far your vision stretches to. Many people would rather just get rid of a problem that they feel the emotional weight of. They can't see further than this, so can't articulate where they want to be instead. Their aim is just to get back on an even keel, as I mentioned previously.

When you are motivated by getting away from something and you allow me to wave my wand, all you can hope for is escapism. You haven't really fixed what was keeping you unhappy in the first place, and so there is a likelihood of ping-back. If I waved a wand and you lost two stone, you would likely find it again, because you haven't done anything to cause it – you've changed no habits and applied no new supporting thoughts. In fact, when you ping back to the original or even greater weight, you will give your ego fodder to judge you with. Things like, 'Yep, I knew she'd never keep that weight off. She was too lazy to exercise so she just got that author woman to wave her wand.'

Once upon a time, when I didn't know myself and I was too emotional to see straight, I constantly looked for evidence that I wasn't good enough. That version of me didn't do well in relationships at all, and I lost a number of friends and loved ones over the years. Luckily for me, the main ones I lost were the ones who told me that my expectations were too high. That I should relax more and lower them if I was to be happy. This is a fundamental lie.

My gut told me that I was worthy. I deserve to have people around me who care about me, who ask me how I am, and stick around to hear my answer. Who aren't jealous of me, who believe me when I say I am feeling scared, and who show up when I need them. Settling for a life where I tolerated anything other than this was not something I wanted.

If you have any kind of fear, then the thoughts, assumptions and expectations that you have in your head about potential outcomes aren't helpful. If you are to give yourself the best chance of success and set a great example for others, what's the point of tying your hands behind your back with disabling thinking? It isn't helpful.

What *would* be helpful is to wear Unicorn Effect lenses and look at the world with positive expectations. Use these expectations to seek new evidence, which will present new opportunities. Lay out a path before you, even though you might not know how to tread all of it. When I drive to the Lake District, my head lights don't light the whole journey, they just light the piece of road directly ahead of me. You don't need to know all the answers, you just need to know what the next step is. Any more information will distract you from the action you are best-placed to take right now.

You don't need all the answers. Often, I meet new clients who have unrealistic expectations of themselves and the world around them. They are waiting to be perfect before they will take action, but this is a sure way to end up taking none. They are making the mistake of assuming they need all the answers when they embark on something new. They can't possibly have them – it's new!

When I had a baby, I didn't know what to do. I had done some learning by looking at other people and reading books, but I largely had to rely on my instincts to do the job. This is a great analogy for leadership. Look at what is in front of you, see what the situation needs, trust that you have what it takes to address that need, and do so with as much love as you have in your heart. If I didn't think this way as a new, or (for that matter) not so new, parent, what hope would I have of bringing up a child? Stepping up begins a journey of real time learning. You quickly see what works and what doesn't as you put one foot in front of the other.

You are already a leader. People are already looking to you to guide them, whether you have the job title or not, so stop being so self-absorbed with all these fears, and show up for them, would you? Do it for the people you care most about and want to leave a legacy for. Own it.

It is easier to stop limiting behaviour in its tracks than it is to continue playing small. As you take new actions, you will become aware of new evidence that lines up with what you want and not with your history. You did that. You created it. Now you can expect more of yourself. Expect that people want to and are desperate to hear what you have to say. Only *you* can say it the way that will make an impact. Believe that. If you operate in this way, and put all of your efforts in the direction of the things you truly want to impact, you will set a superb example of leadership.

One question to ask yourself today:

What if there was no 'right' way to do things?

Part One
Conclusion

Now you have your baseline. You know where you are and why you have felt an inability to progress. I hope that the questions I have posed at the end of each chapter have helped you to realise that you don't need to choose to be stopped by those perceived obstacles any longer. Your thinking is now unlocked, and you are ready to identify what small steps you can take to move towards a simpler, yet bigger, version of you. Take a breath. Ready to be the leader you want to see? Then let's move to part two: Bravery.

PART TWO
BRAVERY

People always comment on how brave I am. I want to show you how I have become that way through building it as a habit. This section is going to bring you increased clarity, as each brave step brings you new information that may adjust your direction. Nothing in this section is going to scare you dramatically. That's not what building a habit is about. You'll see that changes can be small, but continue to make those changes, and you'll see a huge impact on your outcomes.

Unlock The Best You

This section is going to help you get out of your own way. Those obstacles that were in your way were conceptions in your mind. Now is the time to start playing bigger.

11. Responsibility versus blame

'We are 100% responsible for all our experiences. Every thought we have is creating our future.'
— Louise Hay

There are people in your life who are going to trigger you. They are going to say something that you respond to defensively, and the thought their comment generated will send you into a spiral of making everyone else wrong – especially the person who triggered you.

REAL-LIFE EXAMPLE: YOU CAN'T PUT A PRICE ON THAT

I posted a client testimonial on LinkedIn recently, in which she had repeatedly said, 'You can't put a price on that.' I quoted her in the post and referenced that 'I get to' put a price on the service she received. I was coming from a positive place – I didn't want to say, 'I have to', which smacks of obligation. I wanted to acknowledge it as an honour. Unfortunately, one reader read it in a sinister way, as if I was sitting in my house chuckling at how I am making money from the need for transformation. Of course, I am making money from transformation, that is what I do for a living, but that is not what her reaction was about. She was looking inwardly at her own money shame, and her inner soundtrack of self-judgement made her judge me. The good news is that this lady, who was about to start working with me, did one important thing. She didn't stay in a space of making me wrong. Instead, she took responsibility. She recognised her need for help with her money mindset and made a point of telling me it was a place we needed to focus on in our six months working together.

Many people don't take responsibility for their judgement. They stay in the energy of making people wrong. Those people would have judged me, unfollowed me, told people what a money-grabber I was, and just focused on condemning me without inviting another viewpoint. But remember what Wayne Dyer said about judgement? It reflects the person passing it, not the one being judged.

Blaming other people all the time is completely unrewarding. As we know, it keeps us in our own fear of judgement, while also giving our power away.

People committed to blame don't just blame others, they also take the blame all the time. You can spot a blamer easily because they are constantly apologising. If you take the time to look at what they are apologising for, it is normally not an action that is attributed to them. My daughter does this – she says 'sorry' when she doesn't know something is wrong, and the statement she is most affected by is, 'I'm going to tell on you.' All we want to do as children and adults is be good and be thought of as good by others. The best way to achieve that is by taking responsibility, not blame.

My recommendation to take responsibility is not always met with open arms. It can generate one of two reactions:

1. Why should I?

2. You mean it's up to me? Great!

Blamers sit around complaining. They wait for other people to make decisions about their direction. And when they don't get the outcomes they want, they get angry about it.

If you want to make a positive impact in the world, then you need to take 100% responsibility for your life. The people choosing option one aren't doing that. They believe blame and responsibility are synonymous. They are weighed down by obligation and guilt, and often feel unsteady.

The people choosing option two see the opportunity in taking responsibility. They feel relief, as they now see that they can choose how they think, feel about, and respond to everything.

Taking responsibility sets you free. It helps you focus on what you can change, not what you can't.

When someone cuts me up in the car, it makes me angry in the moment. I get righteous about their dangerous driving. But I can't change it. What I can do is make sure that I continue to drive as safely and as vigilantly as possible, so that when it happens (because it will), I am able to avoid a collision. Putting my focus into what the other driver is doing doesn't help me at all.

Stop complaining

> 'When given the choice between being right and being kind, choose kind.'
> — Wayne Dyer, quoted in RJ Palacio, *Wonder*

Complaining drains your energy and damages your optimism. When you complain about people or situations, you are really looking for someone else's agreement to the story. You are seeking to enrol them in the drama of the thing that happened. All that will prove is that you were right. Your ego loves to be right.

Complaining leaves an emotional residue. We often feel guilty afterwards, and this only reinforces our inner critic. To others, we appear untrustworthy and miserable. If you're reading this thinking, 'But my friends agree with me', then you may want to consider new friends. Otherwise, you will spiral down this rabbit hole together and not have a lot to show for it at the end.

EXERCISE: THE ONE-MINUTE ANTIDOTE TO COMPLAINING

This exercise was inspired by my daughter one Christmas when, on opening fifteen or so presents, she chose to focus on the one present she wanted that she didn't get. It brought the energy of the day down and was dismissive of the generosity others had shown. All those images of people less fortunate than us flashed around my head. I wanted her to be grateful for what she had, not miserable about what she believed she didn't have.

We cracked open one of the games and I grabbed the timer. Instead of using it to count how many claps (178) or hops (104) she could do in a minute, we used it to see how many things we could acknowledge that we were grateful for in that time. The whole family did it and it transformed us from sad and disappointed to unbelievably appreciative and connected. As a result of that one minute, our spirits were lifted for the rest of the Christmas period, and we now play that game regularly.

You may not want to carry an egg-timer around with you, but you probably wouldn't be without your phone. Set yourself a one-minute countdown and just think about all the things that you have and are able to do in your life – for example, I can breathe, eat, have food available, move, talk, read – the bar doesn't have to be high. In fact, the lower, the more humble, the better!

Focus on you. Take responsibility for your life and your emotions. When you feel wronged, focus on the remedy, and the emotional energy you can now release.

You're reading this book because you want something to change, and you need help to clarify what actions to take. Well, this is one – take responsibility. Every time you feel yourself complaining about or judging another person, focus on what action you need to take as a result. Maybe your thoughts are reminding you of a promise you haven't kept to yourself, which you now have an opportunity to recommit to.

One brave act today:

What will you choose to be free of today by taking responsibility?

12. Unclench

This always makes me laugh. This concept came about on one of my retreats when the lovely Kate was extremely articulately, as always, describing all the fears that were getting in the way of her being the person she wanted to be. Kate is a phenomenal leader, but she was riddled with self-doubt when I met her. When she felt overwhelmed, she would hold both hands in fists above her head like she was being strung up in some Netflix thriller. I asked her to freeze and got the rest of the group to describe her body language – then someone said '*Unclench!*'

That was it – her new anchor word, and the rest of the people on the retreat. From that moment, Kate had a physical way to spot when the soundtrack in her head was going rogue, when she was telling herself that she couldn't deal with what was going on. She then started a comical journey towards having long fingers in the air, like she was playing a virtual piano, and letting out long meditative outward breaths. She was consciously unclenching. Wiggling her fingers now is enough to remind her to unclench.

Maybe the penny hasn't dropped yet, but I think I know you. You are a control freak. You don't want to make all the decisions or have to be the one that organises everything for your group of friends, yet you want to go to the places *you* want to go to, and you want to go at a time that suits you. I get it. I'm a control freak, too. But if you want to make a big impact in the world, you don't have time to waste on doing it all. You can trade that for the time to guide, teach and influence – much more fulfilling.

First, you need to unclench. Just take a moment and have a look at your life. I know you believe you have a lot on, and I know you think it is all down to you, but doing it all makes you the administrator, not the leader. When you are really organised, have great insights, can see problems clearly and come up with solutions quickly, it is normal to believe that you can do it all, and it is tempting to also *want* to do it all. You are the mother who zips the coat up to get the child out of the house quickly, or the boss who writes the report themselves because the team don't do it quite the way you want it. These acts may save you in the short term, but they have a long-term cost.

Short-term fixes don't make a big contribution. They merely teach you how to cope, while taking away everyone else's opportunity to develop.

This book is about helping you play the long game – it's about thriving, not surviving. The longer you do things for people, the longer you will disempower them from doing it for themselves. They need to learn from you. Show them how great they can be.

If, like Kate, you grip your hands for thirty seconds, you will feel tired. Imagine doing this all day long, and you will begin to see the cost of having such a tight grip on your life. You need to loosen it. Great leaders don't hold on so firmly. They allow the people around them to shine and actively do their best to help to find development opportunities for others. While you are worrying about your own leadership, you are denying someone else a chance.

It takes a brave leader to give other people a leg up. Paul David was this person for me. He was the leader who trusted me to deliver, and gave me opportunities that had my hands shaking with nerves but stretched me beautifully. He saw, long before I did, that to be at my best, I didn't need to work harder in my job, I needed to focus on me, my wellbeing, and even said something about getting a life! He got me my first coach, and that is the reason I am where I am now.

You are going to be the reason that many, many people get to their ideal position. Your actions, considerations and words of support are going to both propel people and slow them down when they need it. But *you* have to be the leader *they* want to see.

Say 'yes'

Allowing yourself to be supported is a major part of staying unclenched. Every woman I know struggles to ask for help. The good news is that your first brave step doesn't involve doing that. It simply involves saying 'yes' when help is offered. You are being offered help all the time, but you are so programmed to reject it, you might not even hear it anymore. Again, keep the bar low, listen out for offers of help and say 'yes' to them all.

When I first got a PA, I didn't know how to work with her. I was utterly self-sufficient and didn't believe anyone could do anything as well as me. I had to let go and educate people to meet my needs. Every time she offered to help me, I struggled with what to say. I decided the best way forward was to come clean. I invested time in letting her see me. She saw how I worked, she saw my intolerance for time being wasted, she saw my attention to detail, and she saw my control freakery. When I invited her to a meeting, I told her I didn't want her to take minutes, I wanted her to come out of the meeting clear on the one thing she could take off my plate. As time went on, I had less and less admin to worry about. She learned my ways of working and pre-empted my needs. She did less chasing and more reminding ahead of deadlines, so deliverables were never late. If I had just kept on saying, 'I'm fine, thanks', I would not have been a leader for the team. I would have been an overpaid administrator. Instead, supported by my PA, I could be the person influencing the decision makers ahead of our board approvals. I was clearing the path, securing resources. I was making a real impact.

When you are offered help, take it. Ask your team and colleagues to look at what you are responsible for and give them permission to take something. They will choose something that feels easy to them – it might not seem the same way to you… When you let them take it, though, really *let* them do it. The worst habit of control freaks is to delegate something, but not actually let it go. Start small – give low-impact tasks away, then gather proof that it is safe and the person can be trusted. Be honest if you are worried about something. Agree what a week-long task is going to look like by Wednesday and check in. Provide support, don't take over.

You can do this at home, too. If you complain to your partner or children about them never helping around the house, and then the minute they try, you take over the task in a huff and do it yourself, what message are you sending? One of mistrust. One of self-importance. That's not leadership.

Lowering your standards is not the solution here – education is. This is what I mean by the long game.

If you like things done a certain way but you want help, then you must clearly communicate how you want them done and why that's important. If you want the washing hung up a certain way, explain that upfront. Of course, you can inject some humour into why you are being so precise, but generally if people know why you're being so specific, they won't judge. It's important to know to peg dresses in the armpit, don't you think? (Pay attention to your reaction to that question!)

If someone puts too much milk in your coffee, say, 'That's lovely, thank you, but a little less milk next time', with a wink. Or, if you want to keep it simple, 'Coffee would be fab, can I have the milk on the side please? Thanks so much.'

I know for sure that there are more people who admire me for being clear about what I want and asking for it than there are people wanting to judge me negatively for that.

Start warming yourself up to communicate what you want. Don't say you don't mind when you do really. There is a spectrum, and you want to be nicely balanced around the middle. You don't want to be dictatorial about everything, and you certainly don't want to settle for things when they are important to you. Define the things you really care about and what things you genuinely aren't fussed about. Make a list. Go on – I'll start.

Things I really care about that anyone in my social or professional circle knows about me:

- Being on time

- Decent wine

- Products used to clean my house (I only realised this when a new cleaner used Dettol to clean my hardwood floors!)

Things that don't bother me:

- The time I need to get up

- What airline I fly with

- Who drives

I'll be honest, it took me a lot longer to come up with the second list!

Get to know yourself and educate others. Set them up to help you get where you want to go. If the chosen seat in the cinema is going to affect your enjoyment of the film, state your preference in advance. It doesn't mean you have to take over the booking. More on this later.

One brave act today:

What will you delegate today?

13. Faking it won't make it

In every talk I give on impostor syndrome, someone asks me what I think of the 'Fake it 'til you make it' approach. I'm astounded that as of 2020, there are still articles advising people to do this, without any caution about the downside of that approach. I'll admit, I have used the phrase myself in the past and I have come to see what terrible advice it is. Someone who is faking it never makes it. They put an awful lot of energy into being a certain way because it is deemed more acceptable. It may even bring results in the short term, but they will never own their success this way.

Faking it until you make it creates a number of problems. Here are just three:

- **It leaves you unable to accept compliments.** If you faked it, if it was a team effort and not all you, then how can you take the praise? If you know that you acted in a way that wasn't true to you, you will feel like a fraud when someone applauds you for it. You'll just reinforce your impostor syndrome.

- **Faking it requires effort and leaves you permanently expecting a pay-off.** And when it doesn't pay off – because it won't, not really – then you will tip into resentment. Resentment is a silent form of anger that dribbles out in communication. It will be seen in looks, eye-rolls, snide comments that hurt just enough to let the other person know you aren't happy with them. It creates this façade that you end up hiding behind, because if you come clean all the other masks you wear will have to come down, too.

- **It is utterly confusing for the people around you** – the people in your life and who you work with. They won't know whether they are coming or going with you, what mood you're going to be in. They will never know if it is safe to talk to you or not.

Fake is false protection

When I was clinging on to my mum on the first day of school, she gave me the only advice she believed in.

In her stern Irish accent, she said: 'Susan, you go in there and you act like the most confident person in the room.' Of course, she was trying to protect me.

I definitely went in there acting, but I'm pretty sure confident is not what it looked like. Picture people at work who strut around like they own the place, thinking that they are oozing confidence. Do you ever admire these people, or do you steer clear of them, believing them to be arrogant? The two things are closely related, and I am convinced that many women choose not to be confident because they are afraid it will be mistaken for arrogance. Truthfully, it probably will be. If you pretend to be someone you aren't, if you are focused on covering up the person you think isn't good enough and try to dupe people into believing things about you that *you* don't believe, you are going to fail. And people may well mistake you for arrogant, as they mistook me.

This fake person cannot possibly connect with other people. She isn't relatable at all. On that first day of school when I was just four, without realising, I probably put distance between me and a number of potential friendships. I don't have that group of friends that I have known since school. Probably because no one knew me at school. I was so busy pretending and trying to get my teacher's approval that I didn't pay attention to all the joy around me. Don't get me wrong, my childhood wasn't miserable, but I do look back and wonder how different it could have been if

I had been encouraged to believe that being scared on that first day was completely normal and acceptable.

I could swap out school for work here and add thirty years to my age and the story would be exactly the same. *Exactly*. I didn't own my confidence at the early stage of my life, and I didn't own it later, either. It wasn't until I was in my mid-thirties and I had worked on my own limited mindset and self-doubt that I realised that there are, in fact, things I am confident about. I didn't need to fake it anymore. As soon as I stopped faking it, I started to see what was truly great about me. Those things didn't require me to try, they just required me to *be*.

When I stopped faking it, I started to create real relationships. I realised it was OK to show when I was sad or hurt. It was OK to communicate my fear. It was OK not to have all the answers. I didn't have to hide my honesty anymore. Truth is the root of connection.

Be your North Star

'Mama, you are Polaris.'
  – Elise Ramroop

This is the feedback my daughter gave to me on a morning walk to school. I had just come back from a conference in Amsterdam, where I had shared the Unicorn Effect concept, and her eyes were wide with pride. This is how she captured how she felt about how I showed up, and the example I set for her as well as those 600 people in the audience. I am the brightest star in her sky. Listen to the feedback that has the best impact on you. Use your self-knowledge as your North Star and know that it is the real you that will make the most effective leader. The one that inspires others.

You can, and might already, be the standout star for your people, too. But with light comes darkness...

When you show up truthfully, you may clash with others. I know I have a number of people in my life who still aren't that comfortable being honest about who they are. When I am vulnerable, their instinct is to try and fix me, or wash away my feelings with their belief in me. While this comes with good intentions, it isn't that helpful.

All we want is to be heard. If we aren't heard, then we don't feel seen, and if we don't feel seen, then we feel insignificant. Then we usually pretend none of that matters by putting on a brave face and 'soldiering on'.

Faking it 'til you make it, soldiering on – it's all ignorance of your true feelings. Those feelings are there to guide you. If you numb them, you won't be able to detect nervous excitement or joy, the two things that are critical to move you to a life of contribution.

Know who you are, and what's important to you. When you focus on these things and all the brilliance they offer, you don't need to spend your time or energy on things you fake. There is plenty of authentic activity to keep you occupied.

So what if you have weaknesses? It is only your focus on them that creates a problem for you. It requires a lot of effort to be mediocre at best. If you focus on your strengths, then you don't need to 'fix' what you perceive to be broken.

Being the truest version of yourself is the goal here. Trusting that you are enough is going to get easier as this book goes on.

One brave act today:

Choose something to be honest about today. Make a note in your diary that no one died as a result!

14. Who are you really?

When we take away all our stalling tactics, all the things that have been distracting us from getting clear, and just allow ourselves to be, well, ourselves, who are we really?

So far, you have believed your identity to be what your inner critic said it was, but I hope you have now realised that it has been lying to you. That is solely the voice of your insecurities and it persistently looks to present you with evidence that it is absolutely right. I am going to shift your lenses to see the truth. Who are you when you aren't trying to please other people or gain their permission? Who are you when the noise of your inner critic is dialled down, and you can connect to how you really feel, and what is going on inside?

I may already have taken you into scary territory here. There was a pay-off to you fogging up your lenses with the noise from the last few chapters. Making other people wrong meant you didn't have to look at yourself. Perhaps you were afraid of what you might see. But remember, you are the person who can take responsibility for that and decide whether or not you like it. Choose then to amplify the good bits and simply don't focus on the bits that aren't serving you.

I found this step of my personal transformation very emotional. The worst part was not a list of things to be ashamed of, or times that I regretted. It was how much time I had wasted.

My true strengths were the things that other people had tried to change over the previous decade. I had let other people's insecurities dictate who I should be, and ultimately it had derailed me. Of course, I had invited that by constantly trying to please them in search of being good enough.

Here's the truth: you have everything you need to be a successful leader and have a huge impact on the world. Once you start cheerleading yourself like you do all your friends, you'll realise how phenomenal you are.

EXERCISE: THREE LITTLE WORDS

If I were to ask your friends to describe you in three words, what would they say? How about the people who you deliver for at work – your internal stakeholders? And what about the people who you meet externally? All those people will have a view, and all of them will have good things to say. Do this exercise with people whose views you trust. You will be amazed by what they tell you.

There are no right or wrong values in life. These isn't a set of wonder values that have been signed off secretly and that only a limited few have. Your values are who you are, what you live by, and how you navigate your world. They become a filter for the people who you spend time with and the environments you choose, and that includes the workplace.

You know who you are – it is time to be honest with yourself.

Find your joy

When you are in a joyful state, you are being the best version of you. The negative emotions of fear, anger or guilt can't operate when you are in this energy. Joy puts you in the best state to serve as a leader. Favour it over the unhelpful patterns we already covered.

You can connect to your joy anywhere, any time – it is a habit you choose. You may believe that you will experience more joy when you get a better job or find a better friend, but, honestly, if you can't experience joy now, you won't experience it then, either! You are in charge of your emotions and can take full responsibility for them. Maybe your current role doesn't bring you joy, but there is joy to be had at work. Find it. Cause it. Be it.

As we know, having a goal that is all about a job title is an ego-led goal. Having a goal that is an emotional state will always have you reach it, long before the thing you thought those emotions depended on. This will not only mean that you reach your peak state much sooner, but it will also guard you against reaching the goal and feeling flat when you get there.

Johnny Wilkinson, England fly-half, achieved all of his goals in his twenties. He thought he'd made it. He went to bed in Australia feeling like the champion of the world and woke up feeling lost. The world was normal. No one was there to carry him around in a sedan chair. He had nothing left to aim for. And without that, he didn't know who he was.

A lot of sportspeople have this feeling post-retirement or injury because their joy was dependent on doing. It's never enough. Make your goals about being more of who you already are. No circumstance can ever take that away from you. Not unless you let it.

Joy comes from doing what we love, connecting to others and being free to be ourselves. Genuine, life-affirming joy is not going to come from buying yourself a new perfume or handbag. Joy is free.

EXERCISE: MAKE A JOY-LIST

Make a list of all the things that put a smile on your face. Perhaps they are things you do when you have time, or maybe you have let them slide over the years.

Now add how long you think you need to extract joy from these activities. Reading, listening to music, and exercising are all examples where people tell themselves they need an hour, for example. Ask yourself, do you need to listen to a whole album, or can you have a playlist of songs that can transform your state with a single track? Do you need to read half the book, or can you grab a chapter at a time while you are in a queue or waiting for the kettle to boil? Do you need to make time to get into the car to get to an exercise class or could you dance around the kitchen doing your Zumba moves?

Once you know how long you need to feel joy, you can start building it into your day – it won't take long, after all. Isn't it better to have joy on tap like this rather than feeling like you never have time and don't know how to make time for it?

Be prepared. Whatever is on your joy-list, make sure it is enabled in your handbag. I never go anywhere without my kindle or headphones. If someone is late, I get extra joy from a podcast or video. I read and write books by being prepared and having the necessary apparatus available to me at all times. Compare this with scrolling through social media again or getting annoyed because you have been kept waiting. Which one will feel better?

Shape your day around what brings you joy. Walking my daughter to school is a significant part of my day that reflects my values and joy. I am outside, I am with the person I love most in the world, I am moving my body, we are connecting through touch and conversation, and when I walk back home, I get clarity about where I am going to focus my time and energy that day. I do the same walk again to decompress in the afternoon. A contribution to my 10,000 steps is a bonus!

Use your values to turn around events that are in your diary. First, look at your social plans. There will be things in there that will trigger more joy than others. Ask yourself what you are most looking forward to and why. *Is* there something to look forward to? Is it full? Is there more space than you would like?

I spent many years going out most evenings, almost as if I was a failure if I stayed in. If someone cancelled plans, I would be elated as by then, I would normally be in desperate need to lounge on my sofa. The question is, why didn't I give myself permission to do that? The answer: I judged sitting on my sofa as lazy. Unproductive. The truth was I gave all my time to work, and so my social life cut into my sleep time, my gym time, and my downtime. Some days I would come in the door, take my coat off, and go straight up to bed. Most days, if I am completely honest. Any wonder I felt lonely, disconnected, tired and stressed?

If I were to look at that same diary now, like you are doing, I would be able to see exactly what didn't belong.

It takes courage to look at how you're spending your time and to physically address it, so you feel better. I realised that there is a tipping point for most things, and a sharp drop-off when there is too much of a good thing. When I studied garden design some years ago, I learned the concept of negative space. If I packed every inch of a garden with shrubs it wouldn't look like a garden anymore – it would look like a wasteland. Your diary is the same. It needs blank space to highlight all the things you have planted there intentionally.

You will notice when something good becomes too much. And you will see when something you need is lacking. After years of running and re-running this process, I am now acutely aware of what happens to my energy and where my tipping points are. Here's what I know:

- If I have more than two evenings out per week, I go from looking forward to them to feeling tired before I have even left the house.

- I can work away from home for max three days a week without being desperate for my home comforts and my own company.

- I need to read, go outside and move my body every day.

- I can't drink alcohol after 9pm and expect to sleep.

Over time, seek to eliminate everything from your diary or daily routine that doesn't bring you joy or that introduces lower energy patterns. That includes going to restaurants where the food isn't delicious, tolerating low-quality items at home, and spending time with people whose values don't match yours.

When you are connected to your joy, people will be drawn to it, and you are likely to be unattractive to the people whose energy could negate it. This requires no conflict. Choose to be led by how you feel. Your emotions are your guide. Don't push them down or numb them by being too busy… nor with your nightly glass of wine!

One brave act today:

Cancel one thing in your diary that you are dreading, without lying.

15. Boundaries

Everyone knows about the conceptual importance of boundaries, yet so many people fail to have them in place. What I think puts people off is the assumption that they are going to be like a prison fence, keeping you in and the world out. There is a fear that if you have boundaries, you will push people away, and that might generate conflict or result in loneliness.

Boundaries are really just a reflection of your values, what you stand for. They aren't something that need to be enforced as much as consistently represented. Boundaries act as a filter for what is and isn't OK with you.

Putting boundaries in place doesn't have to be a big deal that you announce to the world. The aim is to rectify what you have been tolerating and the resentment associated with this. Choose to exit the in-between energy and say 'no more' to the things you are merely tolerating. Start with the thing bothering you the most.

By putting in a boundary to remedy this, you are doing a number of things:

1. Rescuing the energy that you are currently pouring wastefully into the status quo

2. Educating people so that you don't have to defend these boundaries in future

3. Actively choosing the company and environments you spend time in

You will soon gain perspective on where the real problems lie. For example, you might think that the problem you have at work is the company culture, but it may really be your toleration of it. You have two choices – stop contributing to it, or leave. Personally, I favour the former. If you believe this in your current job, you have the capacity to believe it in your next job, too. Once the initial excitement of a new job wears off, you will start to see the same patterns emerge, because they are a reflection of what you have tolerated up to this point.

If this resonates, take a moment and use that to fuel your decision to change. Take responsibility for your role in the patterns you may have observed in the past.

I took a painful look at how my own behaviour might be affecting, or perhaps even reinforcing, the pattern of time-wasting that drove me to frustration on a regular basis.

First, I looked at my life. Despite having been brought up to hold timeliness to the highest esteem, and never being late anywhere (until I had a baby), I used to tolerate lateness from others all the time. If a friend arrived late and said sorry, I'd let them off the hook, yet be mad at them inside my head. But by letting it slide time after time, I was teaching that friend that being late was OK with me. If I had pulled them up on it after seven or eight occasions of being late already, they might have been quite confused. By that point, I would also have been simmering away on it, and would have been highly unlikely to express my feelings calmly, having stored them up all that time.

I then looked at work and the same applied to meetings. My default response to 'Sorry I'm late' was, 'No worries'. Adults, like children, will push the boundaries until they are stopped and re-educated. One day, I announced at a project meeting that from now on, I wouldn't be tolerating lateness. I explained that it is important to me to be on time, and that I saw punctuality as a sign of respect for me and the other members of the team. I made this announcement at the beginning of a project conference call and everyone said, 'Great!' No push back at all. Ten minutes later, someone joined the meeting late and said 'Sorry, Sooz.' And I said, 'No worries!'

I was programmed to be polite. I was programmed to tolerate.

I caught myself and said, 'Actually, Fred – worries! You can listen to the recording, but in short, I will not be recapping any more for people that are late. This meeting will always start on time and I would appreciate you making every effort to be here at the beginning.' He said, 'Of course, I will be from now on. Forgive me.' From that moment, the dynamic of that team changed. I had done the brave thing of asking for a need to be met. It was partly my need, but it had an impact on the productivity and the mutual respect of the wider team, too. Everyone appreciated it.

You see, I am positive that the other people who were on time had been getting frustrated, too. They were looking to me as the chair of the call to lead it well, and I hadn't been. I was playing small. Standing up for my values and creating a boundary that day made a big difference. And it wasn't as scary as I thought.

Did I really think that someone was going to disagree, refuse to be on time? On reflection, that was unlikely. It was also unlikely that lateness would persist. I had made a public declaration and request. No one wanted to be the person called out for being late. I also didn't want to be the one to call that person out, but I didn't have to. Being brave upfront and explaining my reasons why had gone down well.

It felt selfish initially to get everyone to do what I wanted them to. It felt like it could easily be confused for a moment of being a control freak. How do you differentiate one from the other? Well, there were individual and team benefits to doing as I had asked. It was something so basic and simple that it raised the question to others, 'Why am I not here on time?' When the answer was because the previous meeting had run over, it inspired people to encourage timeliness in those meetings, too. By showing other people what was possible, I had given them permission and inspiration to do the same. Ultimately, what I did wasn't self-serving at all. It was great leadership.

Imagine playing a tennis game with no lines, and having the ball be called out. That is the equivalent of unenforced boundaries. People need to be educated on where your boundaries are, given an indication when they are close to the line, and then told when they have gone over it. None of this needs to be a conflict – it just needs to be clear.

When you are communicating your boundary, focus on what you want. It will automatically negate what you don't want, which will no longer need to be voiced. When you have made your positive request, stop talking. If you do voice the negative, it will sound like a complaint. Don't contaminate your clarity.

Remember not to invite rejection by asking 'Is that alright?' or giving people a way out. Speak in clear statements about what is and isn't OK. Check that you have been understood. That's it!

One brave act today: .

Think about one boundary that is being overstepped. Create a sentence that solves it, and then voice your solution today to someone you love.

Leadership Mindset

Now that we know who you really are, we are going to set up your new way of thinking and reveal your true leadership potential. This will make it more straightforward to achieve the fulfilling career you desire.

16. Focus

'Until your one thing is done, everything else is a distraction.'
   – Gary Keller and Jay Papasan

Once you are clear about what you want, a laser focus is what will help you with the small acts of bravery that will get you to your goals.

If I asked you how you spent your time yesterday, over the last week, and over the last month, would I be able to predict exactly what your goal is? Would I see that you were making every effort to achieve the thing that you claim is most important to you in every action you took?

It's unlikely, right?

I apologise if I am doing you a disservice, but everyone I know has a life and it sometimes gets in the way because our behaviours allow it to. Without focus, I might only achieve things related to being a mum on any given week. If I am not taking my daughter somewhere, I am organising something for her. I don't want to end up resentful about this, and so it is important that my needs and goals have their place somewhere in my schedule, too. First place, ideally.

It doesn't matter how much time you believe you have in which to make a difference, provided you are focused during that time. This is much easier when you only have one goal and you have a plan to get you there.

Do you know what your one goal is? What is really going to make a difference to the way that you live your life? What is going to make the biggest impact building a successful and fulfilling career?

My sense is that women especially find this difficult to do. They start to feel guilty about the things that won't get done rather than connect with the joy of getting the goal done. When you achieve one thing that you have been focused on, you will extract so much energy from it that everyone around you benefits. Look at people who have won awards and commendations – they get them for one thing that stood out. This isn't something they worked towards only when they remembered.

Think about the one goal that you would *love* to achieve this year (even if you are reading this in December!) What would you have to park in favour of these goals?

For me right now, this book is my one goal. It means that I want to pour all the energy I have into it to make it the best it can possibly be. It doesn't mean I am neglecting everything else in my life, but I am making wise choices. If I go out late tonight, it will impact my writing session tomorrow morning. I am consistently choosing my book over other options that might bring short-term joy. I am still doing fun things, but I am choosing the ones that energise me.

Are you giving your goals your full focus? Or are you diluting your contribution by making yourself too busy?

When I took on the role of Programme Manager for a global telco, I pooled all of the organisation's projects and counted thirty-three in total. On interviewing the project managers and teams about their progress, they basically said they weren't making any. Many of those people were working on multiple projects – they were spread way too thinly and were constantly required to shift their focus from one topic to another. You could say they had no boundaries in place. Negative energy from one project was polluting another.

I asked them how they would feel if they were given permission to focus on just one thing at a time. They all breathed a massive sigh of relief and described that place as a place akin to utopia. So why hadn't it happened? I had to find out. In my first board presentation about how I was going to turn around the division, I summarised this problem and shared my prediction:

'If we continue as we are, then it will take us something like twenty-seven months to finish ten projects. The other twenty-three are unlikely to come to fruition before market conditions change, which means that the business cases won't provide a return on investment. The alternative approach is that we can get 65% of the revenue from five projects and finish them in nine months *if* we choose those five projects now and park the rest.'

I put a lot of work into demonstrating that point and the pressure was all on me to deliver against my proposal. What do you think happened? They hired a Big-Four consulting company to do the same piece of work over the next six months. They lost six months and a lot of cash because they didn't believe what I said.

That was a powerful learning curve for me.

How could it have been avoided? Engaging the consulting company showed me that the board were practised in, and prepared to accept, delays. I asked myself, as the programme manager, why didn't I just take leadership? Why did I ask permission?

Don't ask questions you don't want the answers to.

I was confident that the consulting company would draw the same conclusion as I did, so I figured that they had bought me six months of below-the-radar time to get the work done the way I wanted. No more asking permission.

I explained to the project teams that there would be a new and focused approach for the next six months. When I asked, 'Is there a reason you can't do this today?' I no longer felt like I was pushing. The project teams finally understood that I wasn't asking them to do more, I was asking them to *only* do *x*. They knew I was looking for the thing that was distracting their focus so I could remove it.

EXERCISE: CHECK YOUR FOCUS

You can check the power of your focus by asking yourself the following questions:

- Are you clear on your number one priority?
- Are you making a contribution to it every day?

- Are you getting lost in the process, or are you focused on the result?
- Are your actions intentional – do you have a clear and positive expectation of your actions?
- What are your actions for? Why do they matter?
- What are you specifically here to do? And why can only you do it?

The last one is a big question, and one that I want you to ponder over time.

These are questions that can take you out of the detail when you are feeling lost or overwhelmed. The number one obstacle in the way of your goals is distraction. This can be counteracted quickly by refocusing, narrowing your gaze and excluding all else, even if just for twenty-five minutes at a time.

When I am teaching my daughter techniques for sport, so much of it is about focus and the direction you are pointing towards. When ten-pin bowling, to get a spare, you have to end your motion with your hand pointed towards the target pin. When you hit a tennis shot, your shoulder should point where you want the ball to go. In ball sports the simple reason people don't play well or do so inconsistently is because they take their eye off the ball. It is the first rule. Decide on your ball and watch it at all times. This focus will filter out all other noise and distractions.

If you are struggling to prioritise, use the MoSCoW tool: what must, should, could and won't get done?

When you practise focusing on what you want, your focus muscle will be flexed everywhere. Your family will benefit, your friends will benefit and, more importantly, you will feel like you are showing up as a person who actually makes an impact. Compare this with the overwhelmed person with the long list who barely ticks anything off it.

Focus is the answer to every problem.

One brave act today:

What is the one thing that you would love to do if you could park everything else? Why not choose this as your focus for the next three months? Go on, be brave.

17. We teach people how to treat us

Whether you have dropped your habit of judgement or not, this still applies. People are making decisions about you all the time. It doesn't mean they are judging you negatively, but they are making judgement calls, which are different. Are you my sort of person? Do you make me laugh? Are you someone I can learn from? It is a constant assessment process, when you think about it.

When I meet someone networking, I am listening out for information that might indicate that they have the same values as me, the same ambitions, or perhaps they have achieved what I would love to achieve. My listening is attuned, and if there is no match, I will move around the room until I find the one person who is going to ignite my senses in some way.

People are making decisions about you right now. What information are providing to inform them?

If you are settling for good when you could be great, people will either hear that you are someone who settles or they will just assume that 'good' is the standard by which you measure yourself, and therefore your impact.

My tennis serve is currently average. If someone plays me at tennis today, they may well deduce that I have a weak serve. The ball goes over the net and lands within the lines consistently, but it is unlikely to be an ace. If I'm then spotted having a tennis lesson and I am learning how to serve, they are going to have a different view of me. They are going to expect me to get better at some point and they are going to deduce that I care enough about my game to pay my serve some attention.

If you are the person who never speaks up at work, then you suddenly start speaking up, people are going to notice. They are going to pay attention to you getting more confident. If you tell them that you read the TEDx book about how to give a great presentation, they are going to expect you to be speaking at the next internal conference or representing your company at an industry event. By raising your own expectations, you raise other people's. You get on their radar. People will think of you for promotions, even though you might not have reached the goal yet – they will make a judgement call based on your intentions and your focus, not necessarily the experience you've gained.

Your focus will inspire other people to think, 'Well, if she can do it, perhaps I can, too.'

None of this is about you having reached the goal already. You have taught people that you are focused, committed, and likely someone who is motivated by progress. They are buying into your intentions. I have been hired as a speaker because of a listing at an event – I haven't even delivered the talk or gotten great reviews yet. They have made a decision about me based on what I plan to do.

Language is a significant factor in teaching people how to treat us. I can tell what a person is thinking by the language they use. There are certain words that are revealing. It doesn't make them wrong, but I want to draw your attention to the energy behind them.

Based on my values and my style, which is focused, logical, and mostly optimistic, I like to take the most direct route to the things I want. When I feel overwhelmed or under strain, I don't perform at my best. I prefer steady to all guns blazing. The latter has a habit of tapering off, and I want to remain consistent where possible.

Compare these two statements about an entrepreneur running their business:

1. I'm going to smash my goals this year, because I'll keep on pushing. I haven't got time for holidays or a social life, but I'll have to suck that up.

2. I read a book about taking seven years to reach a million pounds in revenue and I really related to it, so I am following the model and aiming to double my income this year to stay on that trajectory. Here's how I'm doing it.

Which do you relate to more?

For me, the first one spells danger. 'Smash' tells me that this person perceives obstacles that require her to be in combat mode, armed and ready to fight. It requires an awful lot of energy that might not be sustainable for the long term. 'Push' is one of my least favourite words, ever since I studied hypnobirthing – you don't force a child into the world, you allow it to come into the world naturally (where possible). Pushing, unless you are talking about a door, is negative language. Using it will teach people that you buy in to struggle, that you might overthink and overcomplicate things. Pushers are caught in their heads a lot of the time and miss the moments of connection. Lastly, there is an assumption of necessary tolerance in this statement. The belief that you have to suck up whatever you are dealing with is a danger to mental health. Never suck something up. If an emotion or need is rising persistently, listen to it. These warning signs will only last so long before Mother Nature takes over and you are stopped by illness or even a broken relationship.

If you don't take a stand and value yourself, other people won't value you either. And nor will you teach them to value themselves.

Respect your own wishes. Represent them. Decide who you want to be and be the leader they want to see. Stop using the phrase 'I don't mind'. Don't pretend you don't mind when you really do. Or perhaps you genuinely don't mind. Be aware, though, that it is an easy phrase to use when you want to avoid conflict or upset. Instead ask, 'Do you have a preference?' It might generate the same outcome, but it is teaching people to choose positively rather than settle. There are opportunities all around to reframe in this way. Practise making affirmative decisions. It shows great leadership. We will talk more about this in part three.

One brave act today:

**Choose to be affirmative today
over sitting on the fence.**

18. Why take a leap when you can just stretch?

When I first started my full-time coaching business, I put together a telesummit called 'Taking a Leap'. It was named after a phrase I heard a lot, and it mirrored how I felt about what was required of me to get from where I was then to where I wanted my business to be. I interviewed seventeen people about the concept, people who I believed were further ahead on the journey than me. I wanted to share the lessons with my growing community, but I also wanted to help myself.

A lot of advice was delivered from that interview series, and a lot of it I didn't follow straight away. It is as relevant now as it was in 2016. What I realised with nearly every interview was that I had this impatient corporate pace about me. I was used to darting off in a single-minded fashion because I was doing things I'd done time and time before. Now I was on a new journey, and I didn't know if the direction was right, so I had to get informed first.

I concluded quickly that taking a leap wasn't required, and it could in fact lose me time overall. This was an epiphany. Taking a leap when you are at the beginning of your journey to bettering yourself and creating a greater impact feels big and scary. It creates this fog over your vision, and the courage required to take a leap just seems unfathomable. It sends you surging into all the patterns that I made you aware of in part one of this book. Navigating your way out of those patterns alone feels like hard work. No wonder I was struggling.

The key to getting to where I wanted to go, and making sure it was the right place this time was to take a step and see how it felt to bump up against the edge of my comfort zone.

Picture a child who is learning to walk. They put their foot out just a little bit further than where they are now to check that the ground is safe, and then take the step, expecting that they may topple over. They have already assessed the stability of the ground, so the step then doesn't feel so risky. Each time they get up and have another go, they are more informed than the time before, and as a result the edge of their comfort zone stretches. It's the same for you. Moving yourself forward towards your bigger, more impactful vision, doesn't need you to leap to get there. It's more of a stretch. At this pace, you can easily repoint your arrow if it is aiming a little off course. At my corporate pace, I'd have been long gone, missing all the lessons on the way, and not giving myself the chance to reassess my direction. There is no real expansion available from this viewpoint.

You have everything you need already. You just may not have flexed the muscles in a while, maybe even since you were the toddler I described. If you think about it, taking these 'baby steps' consistently is much faster than the time spent agonising over taking leaps. That image has you standing still for quite a long time, before covering the same distance, *if* you even take the leap, that is. Many people spend so long in fear that they feel paralysed and actually never make progress in the direction of their goals – they simply talk themselves out of it, kidding themselves that it might not be what they want after all.

I don't want that to be you. Getting you to lead all the people who can only be influenced by you is too important. Be the leader you both want to see.

Now you know that your next action doesn't require a leap, I bet much of your fear has dissipated, and all because of a new concept that your mind entertained. Nothing out there in the big wide world changed...

Look for nervous excitement

You can go from being deeply fearful to nervously excited in a single thought. Nervous excitement is an emotion that everyone can recognise. It is very different from fear. It has you grinning, eyes wide with an enquiring 'Can I really? Shall I?' look on your face. This is the target emotion for all your small acts of bravery that are required by this part of the book. It's how you know that what you are about to do is a step in the right direction. Seek this feeling out.

The example I used with Kate in our first session was to run the Mum's race on sports day just two hours later. On the surface, she appeared to be dreading the thought. Deep down, she knew she could do it. It wasn't a terrifying concept; part of her was curious to see whether she'd get a place in the top three or not. This was enough to 'have a go'.

You'll know when you have gone too far when fear has begun to take over. Terror relates to goals that feel too far away – they aren't within your grasp, which means you are unlikely to take timely action. The gamble feels too big, perhaps because the direction is wrong.

Nervous excitement is different, because you are considering rather than ruling out; moving towards, not away from. You are entertaining the idea. You aren't sure if you can do what you're aiming for, but you're excited enough to try.

This is a feeling I try to generate when I run my retreats at Center Parcs. There are a number of opportunities there that make people nervous before they reach the childlike joy stage. Waterslides are a great example. Most women over forty need to have a talk with themselves before they do something like that. First, they have to overcome the inner soundtrack of how they look in a swimming costume, and then they need to contend with the height of the slide and the fact that they have absolutely no control over the pace of the raft. Time and time again at these retreats, I have women hugging me because of the absolute thrill of letting go and enjoying themselves like children. Throwing yourself into something like this gets you out of your head and your comfort zone. It gives you evidence that you *can* do it, and that when you try something that makes you nervous, it can have a massive pay-off.

Listening to the shrieks and seeing the smiles as people come down that slide is priceless. Watching someone feel brave and untouchable, and then seeing their openness to more brave actions as a result is a privilege.

As you get braver, you get more aware, and before you know it you have totally surpassed where you ever thought you would be.

Stretching the edges of your comfort zone and benefitting from its expansion is much easier than forcing yourself outside of it all the time. Some of the stretches that my clients have taken might seem tiny to another person, but to them they represented significant wins. The best thing about taking a stretch is that most other people aren't paying attention to the changes you're making, so there's no pressure on you to perform to any standards.

When Galia concluded she was going to write her first article on LinkedIn, she was excited, but she wasn't all that nervous. When I asked her when she would do it by, she responded 'Two weeks.' *Ahhhh,* I thought. She was in her comfort zone. I said, 'Really? I was thinking more like in the next two hours.' Changing the timeframe made her nervous, and it was exactly what she needed to reach the ultimate proof point of elation that very day. She could have added something to her to-do list to make her busier, created confusion the more she over-analysed it, then ended up in in-between energy about what to write. Instead, she made a decision, took fast, imperfect action, and reaped the energetic reward (see Resources).

If the last two pages had been about taking leaps, you'd have been too stressed out to have taken in what I just said. Don't waste time agonising, look for the action steps that make you nervous *and* excited – they're the ones to take. They lie right at the edge of your comfort zone, not beyond it. And they are available to you today too…

One brave act today:

Do something that makes you squeal with nervous excitement. If you can't think of something, get a friend to suggest it…

19. Go first

If you're anything like me, you have lots of ideas: things you'd love to do, and most of them are followed by a 'but…' The 'but' comes from your head, and it is the thing that is trying to keep you safe. It wants to be rational. In other words, it wants to talk you out of all the fun stuff.

There are so many things that I have done in my life that I am proud of. But there are also so many things I didn't even start because I allowed myself to talk myself out of it long before I got to step one.

When we have a habit of doing this, we also seem to invite the same from other people. We ask for advice in the hope that they talk us out of it. Then we say, 'You're right', and take no action. It means we never get to experience half the excitement available to us at any given moment.

REAL-LIFE EXAMPLE: BONITA NORRIS

In 2020 I had the privilege of listening to Bonita Norris speak – a bright young woman in killer heels, and a new mum to boot. Listening to her speak humbly from her heart made me melt with admiration as she talked about her incredible experience of getting to and climbing Everest, aged just twenty-two.

Before she even began to speak about the climb, I was impressed by the resilience she showed in raising enough money to do the climb. What struck me was the curiosity in her passion. She was so clear about wanting to see the curvature of the Earth from one of the world's highest points that this become her 'soul' focus. Her motivation was clear. In five months, she made a thousand calls asking for sponsorship to get her there, each one resulting in a resounding no. And one day she decided to go on the radio and do one last appeal, at which point someone who had already said 'no' came forward and said 'yes'.

She could have let herself be stopped in so many ways. Listening to her own soundtrack – 'People from Wokingham don't climb mountains like Everest' – or her mother, who kept reminding her, 'You're so clumsy; you'll die.'

Throughout Bonita's story is a common thread: always keeping things as simple as possible, and creating evidence that she can succeed. Contrary to what you may believe, 'reality is kinder'. What we think might happen in our heads is often the worst possible version. Yes, she could have died, but the reality is that taking one step at a time over and over again seemed like a low-risk way to frame the climb.

On the day she was to climb to the summit it appeared that she wasn't going to be physically able. It is this quote that not only got her to begin, but which kept her going until she reached the top of Everest: 'The hardest step is the first one – outside the tent.'

Just take the first step towards what you want. That's the hardest one. After that, you are on your way, and each next step creates momentum and relative ease compared to the last.

What if every time you had an idea, you took a step towards achieving it? Treat everything like an experiment to see if it is worth pursuing. Make that decision based on what looks and feels right to you, and then use the data it creates, as well as your other experiences, to see if it is a goer or not.

Perhaps your idea might sound so hare-brained that you think no one will go for it. You don't see anyone around you who has done it before, and so you think it can't be done. This is the sphere of the entrepreneur. They are looking for ideas that no one has had before – they want to and are willing to be the person who goes first. Maybe there has never been a woman in your firm who has ever made it past management level. Maybe everyone at the top of the business fits into one mould. Maybe you're the only mother in your circle who appears to have big goals. Be the entrepreneur and leverage the opportunity to go first.

Going first brings so much freedom. No one has set the standard, and you bring relief to everyone else who is praying that they don't have to. If you are in a meeting or presentation, be the person who asks a question. It doesn't have to be clever – speak from your heart. Ask for clarity if you don't understand. I ask basic questions all the time and other people always thank me for it. Be the person other people wish they could be. Go first.

If more women had this attitude, there might be more women at the top. Assume that the reason you aren't at your top is because you haven't been spotted yet. Going first will get you spotted, fast. People will start to rely on you and trust you are the person who is happy enough in their own skin that they don't need to wait for an example to be set for them. You are setting your own.

It isn't helpful to believe that women aren't wanted at the top and that is why they aren't there. When I was in that position, it was helpful for me to believe that the reason there hasn't been a woman at the top is that one hasn't possessed the talent that I have – so I'll go first. That may sound arrogant, but I chose to believe what would most help me. By doing so, I stayed in action. Choosing to believe what other people believed would have capped my career at a level that would not have showcased my talent.

What are *you* going to believe?

Going first against all these largely untrue assumptions means that if you mess up, you are no worse off. There are zero expectations. But the minute that you do something positive, you will stand out in a sea of sameness. Be bold. What have you got to lose?

One brave act today:

Put your hand up and ask a question, or thank the presenter for the impact they made on you.

20. Resilience

When I first started my full-time coaching business, I wasn't quite as enlightened as I am now. The first thing I did was not, in fact, to find a way to contribute.

My first action was to embark on finding out where I was inadequate. I read a book called *GRIT*, which my coach at the time recommended, and I did its test. It showed me that, while I had strengths, I also lacked massively in one key area – resilience.

I understood the impact of not being resilient, because I had seen it and experienced it. If the smallest thing happened that signalled things weren't going exactly to plan, I would lose confidence, and with it, my focus. I would get disheartened and distracted by my emotions for days, making bounce-back extremely difficult.

I didn't understand at the time how to develop this, and despite hiring a number of coaches, no one seemed to be able to show me.

Having now run a number of workshops on the topic for high-performing companies as well as for junior doctors and consultants in the NHS, I see that there is some shame around the topic. When people finally pluck up the courage to voice their concern about workload, or convey their feelings about their stress levels, they are not being met with empathy or kindness. Instead, they are being told they need greater resilience. Like me at the beginning of my career as an entrepreneur, they are not being offered any advice as to how to achieve this, and so they feel tossed aside, and left to work it out on their own. The people doing the tossing, of course, have no idea how to help. They are probably feeling their own form of stress and worrying about their deputies is tipping them into overwhelm. Luckily, you are reading this, and I can help.

In every workshop I run, people know that by the time you have reached this emotional state, building resilience is not something you feel capable of doing. It is too late at this point to do anything about it. What people tell you sounds a lot like 'suck it up'.

In my view, resilience is a characteristic, not a technique. It is built through practice, and at no point should be used to suck things up, but rather to reframe. You cannot reframe when you are stressed out to the point of anxiety.

If you look up the definition of resilience, it is about recovering quickly from something that has already happened. If you talk to some of the top sports coaches, they may refer to it as mental toughness. For the purposes of you, your life and your career, I want you to think of it as perspective. Throughout this book, I have been opening your eyes so that you can focus on what counts and reframe the things that appear to be derailing you from your goals. As you get more aware and braver in your actions, this will become second nature to you, and so the need for you to be resilient as an afterthought becomes unnecessary.

If you go through life letting every little thing affect you, it will keep you in a low-energy state and susceptible to stress. If, however, you can reframe quickly or, at the very least, flood any negativity with optimistic thoughts and feelings, then you are going to deal with situations in real time, and not carry negative energy from one situation to the next.

Let's look at an example. Something happens on the way to work, like someone cuts you up in the car, or jumps the queue in Costa, and these things generate a little anger. So when you arrive at work in a rush, only to find the first meeting has been cancelled, you are likely to react adversely. If, however, you think that the driver in front of you is trying to get to the hospital to see a loved one, that the person in Costa is so distracted that they didn't even notice the queue, and the meeting being cancelled is a gift, your mood will be significantly better. Clearly, I am not an angel and nor are you, so you might not be able to do this as often as you like without trying, but you can practise it. Experiment with it – see how actively reframing everything impacts your day. Trust me, it will. You will be kinder to everyone around you, and your loved ones will notice. More importantly, you will be kinder to yourself, and when you do that, everyone benefits, especially the people following your lead.

Everything in your life is happening on purpose. It is *for* you. There are gifts all around. Your job is to deduce how they count towards making every day great, and to achieving what you want.

Operating in this way completely repackages how we view resilience. Formerly a throwaway word used as a reaction to stress, now it has become part of how you show up.

Reframing is just part of the picture, though. Remember we talked about blank space?

Give yourself a break

Your life cannot be comprised only of occurrences and actions – there needs to be some blank space. This is how your tank is refilled, and you can find the balance you seek.

Compare the need for resilience with that craving you get for a holiday. 'I need a holiday' is a telling statement. It means you have not been replenishing enough on a regular basis.

Maybe you are going to work, then straight to an evening class, the gym, or the theatre. Maybe you have a full diary every weekend. While this may help you win a popularity contest, it will also fast-track you to exhaustion.

Replenish little and often. Maybe you can go away for the weekend with friends, but it doesn't all have to be timetabled. It can include reading and noticing the background noise. For me, the ultimate replenishment is having a day a week at least where I don't have to look at my watch. No meetings, no client work, no school run, just me and my senses. I can observe what is going on in the world – sitting in a café people-watching, or even better, sitting on a sun lounger watching the waves come and go, or taking a leisurely walk along a harbour wall.

Give yourself a break. Allow some blank space. If this fills you with fear and anxiety about how you'll have to completely change your diary, start with ten minutes a day.

REAL-LIFE EXAMPLE: TEN MINUTES A DAY

Cristina was always in a rush, permanently stressed, and constantly ignoring signs from her body about the need to slow down. When I suggested she start taking ten minutes a day for herself, I am sure she would have thumped me if it hadn't been for the fact we were coaching over video conference!

Ten minutes a day is nothing to find, but everything to benefit from when you are a person who believes you have no time. Ten minutes a day can be taken back from scrolling, snoozing in the mornings, waiting for someone who is always late, queuing. If you really look at where your time is being wasted, you will see hours and hours where you could be making a bigger contribution. But going from crazy busy to this might be too big a step, so start by telling yourself that rushing doesn't help. When I ask my daughter to hurry up, she immediately gets overwhelmed, and slows down. We are the same. When you are rushing, nothing changes but your mindset. You won't get there quicker, there is still the same traffic, the same train timetable. Going with them instead of fighting against them is step one.

When Cristina slowed down, she noticed that the world stayed the same, but her outlook, and her well-being drastically improved. With this evidence banked, she started to get off the bus one stop earlier and walk. She progressed to going into a shop to look around on the way home, to having a coffee with a magazine on her own, to going to the cinema with no plan, and just seeing the next show.

Spending time alone and slowing down the pace will bring so many other benefits that you will at some point conclude that you can't afford not to take that time. Like Cristina, you will go from a place of having no time to yourself and being susceptible to stress, to keeping boundaries in place that serve your resilience.

When I used to go out for coffee in my fast-paced job, people couldn't understand how I had time. But that walk to the coffee shop gave me the mental space I needed. It put things in perspective. It connected me with nature. I felt important, valued. And when I came back to the office, I was at least twice as quick at making decisions and briefing the team. My space and clarity earned me productivity. I didn't lose time, I just used it a lot more wisely. And when stresses ran high, as they often do in technology innovation, I was starting from a much better place.

Create evidence that taking time for yourself serves you and makes you a better leader. You'll become the person people want on their team – resilience breeds.

One brave act today:

Decide to take ten minutes longer today doing something for you. If you feel inspired to take yourself on a date, do that!

Part Two
Conclusion

If you have been taking all of these actions, I don't need to tell you how you're feeling. You have lifted yourself out of the unhelpful patterns of behaviour and thought, got yourself in motion, and feel like you are making progress towards being the best version of you. This is what fulfilment looks like. Nothing around you really needed to change. You've simply made a choice to be the leader you want to see.

When you practise creating awareness, then addressing those areas with small acts of bravery, you are going to expand your comfort zone for sure. You will now believe that you can do more than you thought you could. Given how capable you were already, that makes you pretty epic! Now let's really pick up the pace in Part Three: Contribution.

PART THREE
CONTRIBUTION

Now you are starting to look remarkably consistent. Being a tiny bit braver has become the norm, and expectations are that you will now always show up in this way. This is where you will build the self-trust that will keep you going when old patterns try to creep back in. They'll try their best, but you'll know what to do…

When you put together everything you have learned so far, that's when you can make it count. This is the fun part where we get tactical in order to achieve the biggest impact.

Build Trust

In order to keep going, you have to build trust in yourself, trust that you can be the leader you want to see. People follow people they trust.

21. Practice makes...

'Practice makes perfect' is the single biggest lie I remember being told throughout my life. It is an expectation that is impossible to meet. When you think about perfection, you can probably have a go at defining it. But if I told you to go about attaining it, it would be a whole different concept.

Aiming for perfection sets you up for judgement and disappointment when you fail.

There have been many books written on the curse of perfection. Women for as long as time have suffered from perfectionism. I don't know why men are never associated with the term, and to be honest, I am not that interested in exploring that within my precious pages! What I am interested in is giving you some perspective and a way of framing perfection that is more helpful to you.

Perfection is a moment in time. The ping of the ball as it comes off the sweet spot of the racket, the perfect note sung or played. That moment that you hit a gold move on 'Just Dance' on the Wii, or is that just me? A perfectly timed comment that generates laughter at a speech, catching someone's emotion that they were attempting to hide and giving back a loving look of support. These are moments in time that connect. They are not about reaching a point of ongoing accuracy.

Think about a child, whether you have one or not. Imagine bringing them up in a world where nothing can go wrong. In that world, there can be no competition because everyone is perfect. In my mind, I start to see images of *The Handmaid's Tale* – uniform looks and behaviour, and absolutely no freedom.

Perfection not only becomes something unattainable for the normal person, but a bland and stifling experience. Through this lens it isn't even that desirable – let's dump it as a concept.

I prefer the phrase 'Practice makes progress'. For me, for my clients and, I am sure, for you, progress is a great motivator. When you feel overwhelmed, it's because you aren't making any progress. When you feel stuck, it's because you aren't getting anywhere. When I initially talk to prospective clients, the thing that stops them from committing to work with me has little to do with me. The issue is that they don't trust themselves to do the work and get the results – they have no track record to rely on. They have spent so long targeting perfection that they have not even started many of their goals. It is impossible, then, to make progress, which leaves them feeling unmotivated and stalled.

REAL-LIFE EXAMPLE: MARGINAL GAINS

The British Cycling team dominated the sport by exploiting 'marginal gains', a concept covered in *Black Box Thinking* by Matthew Syed. Their ultimate goal was to make their bikes go faster. With the help of Dave Brailsford, they have shown that small, consistent, and incremental improvements can make a huge difference when those improvements are aggregated. It works in any process. So why doesn't everyone do it?

Start small

'It is easy to overestimate the importance of one defining moment and underestimate the value of making small improvements on a daily basis.'
— James Clear

We are often so focused on an overwhelming goal that we take our eye off the inputs that will affect that change we seek. I know that the best way to strengthen my back is to do the glute exercises prescribed by my physio. I could focus on my back, but that is more likely to send me into negative energy about my pain. Instead, if I focus on the thing I can do – my input, I start to build trust that this will contribute to the thing I want, which is a stronger back.

Progress can be defined as 'better than before'. If you continually do things better than before, you are going to create momentum in your results, and hence in your attitude and your level of optimism. In other words, what you are putting energy into is paying off in some way. It is making a contribution.

I remember a scene from the TV programme *Madam Secretary*. The youngest daughter was stuck in a pattern of inaction because she found the idea of completing her fashion project utterly daunting. Her Dad asked her what one thing was that she could do to contribute today and she responded, 'I could hem a sleeve.' The idea of hemming a sleeve isn't daunting – it is something that can be done in a moment. The thing is, once the pins are out and one sleeve is on, you'll think you might as well do the other one, then something else. Before you know it, the whole dress is hemmed.

Whenever I feel overwhelmed, I set a timer for twenty-five minutes. It is a reasonable enough length of time to make an impact on a task, and not so long that you can't fit it in. I do this for tidying the house, writing a magazine article, making an important phone call. If you feel like you aren't making progress, try this. Invariably, when the timer goes off after twenty-five minutes, I keep going. By then, my progression muscle memory has kicked in. My energy is higher when the timer goes off, so I finish whatever I am doing to completion. If you feel like you are plateauing on a task, leave it and set a twenty-five-minute timer for something else that is important to make an impact on. Use the momentum from that thing to fuel your bigger, more important goal.

You can apply this to so many tasks. I used to have a fear of sales and, more importantly, client follow-up. I didn't want to reach out to a potential client in case they rejected me – that was the truth. And so, I chose in-between energy over the clarity of getting an answer and moving on.

When we take action, we are by default making progress. If and when I do reach out to someone and they say no, typically we have a great conversation – that conversation in itself makes me feel more connected, and so that is progress. I can also mark them as someone I can release from my to-do list and brain space. If they say 'yes', something new happens. Celebrate the clarity and notice the energy that brings. Use it to free you or propel you. Make either outcome work for you.

Practically, the best way to create progress is to limit the number of distractions you have. When I ask my retreat attendees to create a plan, what they typically do is generate a list of tasks. But a list is overwhelming. An 'order of work', by contrast, is not. I call this incremental action planning. Action one on the list is foundational – it is the thing that is necessary before you can begin any of the other actions on the list. Number two can only happen when number one is complete. Creating boundaries between the tasks like this means that when you are working on action one, you don't need to worry about the rest of the plan. You know for sure that action one will lead you to action two, and when you have completed it you can give your full focus to action two. When you create dependency like this in your plans, you can't not make progress.

If you only do one thing today that makes an impact:

Choose a small thing you can do today that contributes to your focus, and set a timer to get it done.

22. Why willpower won't work

This was a concept that I came across in 2017, and it made so much sense to me. I put together all those

New Year's resolutions that just died a death four days into January due to my lack of willpower. I gave myself such a hard time and created such an unhelpful soundtrack in my head because of it, it made achieving anything an uphill struggle.

Before we even focus on willpower, we have to look at all the things that we have seen in this book already – who are we really, what is important to us, *therefore* what are the goals we are passionate about and committed to achieving?

In July of 2017, I did a consistency challenge in my Facebook group. I realised how important consistency was, and I thought I would use exercise to expose my own patterns in never feeling like making those follow-up calls to prospects or asking if I could speak at a conference. I realised that I spent an awful lot of time in my head negating all the things I said I wanted to achieve. The outcome was that I didn't ever feel like I achieved anything, yet I felt I was working incredibly hard.

The truth is, I was busy, but I wasn't doing anything that was making a difference to the goals that I made out were really important. I was distracted by a need for willpower to get me through, and constantly in fear because I had no real track record of having any.

For thirty-one days in July, I committed to doing exercise live in my Facebook group. Every. Single. Day. I thought maybe it would be like a New Year's resolution, where the first couple of days would be a breeze and then I'd slacken off. No – the brutal reality hit me on day one, and day two, and day three, and so on. I slept badly the night before the first day. I was tired, I didn't want to do it, I looked awful so didn't want to be on camera, and the hours that day went on, and on, and on. I ended up showing up for people in the evening. Luckily, I had been transparent about the experiment and agreed to be 100% open about my own mindset challenges, but it made me realise the level of commitment required to be consistent in everything you do.

In short, I didn't feel like doing exercise on any given day, and so I had to focus on something bigger than me. I had to do it for the other people that had no track record of keeping their commitments to themselves. Some people were doing the same exercises, so I had to show them what to do. I couldn't leave that until 9pm, as they might have gone to bed. I leveraged my habit of being a people-pleaser to show up, because at the time I could rely on it.

Willpower won't work, but habits will. You can't rely on a habit to exercise every day if you don't have a habit of doing that yet.

In 2018, I did a Beachbody programme called '80 Day Obsession'. It was a programme that had a profound effect on me. For the first time in my life, my thighs didn't touch, I was eating broccoli and sweet potato for breakfast, and I was doing some form of exercise

– hard exercise – every day for eighty days straight (with stretching on Sundays). If I hadn't done that initial consistency challenge, I would have had no evidence to suggest that I could do this programme. On the surface, it was about physical transformation, but it is fundamentally a mindset programme that builds a belief of not quitting and creates a ton of evidence that 'I *can*'.

Willpower has nothing to do with your consistency. It is all in the commitment and ongoing courage that you display with your single-minded focus. People judged me the entire time I was doing the Beachbody programme, from the mums in the cinema when I chose sweet potato and green beans over popcorn, to when I asked friends to meet me later so I could eat at home. Most people want to keep you just as you are. They don't share your commitment or motivation yet, but I can tell you that the most cynical of people are watching you like they watched me. Their judgement and jealousy is just a reflection of them. By showing up as a leader in whatever area you choose, they are going to feel like you have shone a light on something they wish they had the courage and commitment to do. Once they get past this, they will be inspired by everything that you remained resolutely committed to, and it will help them change their life at some point. One of the most cynical of my mum friends who eventually admitted she didn't want it enough at the time has now completely transformed her own body. I know that my leadership in this area was the beginning of that thought process for her.

Your leadership helps. This is not about you dragging yourself kicking and screaming through your goals, it is about you being clear about what you want and why, and committing to yourself daily to keep going until you get it. That means not going to bed until you have made a contribution.

Decide what you want and commit

When I was writing this book, I committed to writing every day. While I had a target of writing 1,000 words a day, I allowed myself some flexibility in my discipline. As long as I wrote a paragraph, I could say I'd honoured my commitment to myself. Invariably when you write one paragraph, ten more follow, but it was the secret to getting this book written within the timeframe I promised. There was no willpower involved.

Keeping your word to yourself is the most powerful commitment of all. When you do what you say you are going to, you build a catalogue of evidence that you can do it, that you are reliable, trustworthy. When you have this under your belt, it doesn't matter about the action that gained it. Whether it was exercise or just taking a vitamin every day, knowing that you will stay committed, no matter what, is like a muscle in your mind: the more you flex it, the stronger it gets.

Willpower doesn't work, because it's based on you consciously or unconsciously asking yourself whether you feel like doing something. As my coach, Shanda

Sumpter, said, 'I don't care how you feel. I care that you finish.' Brutal, but effective. Your commitment will work, though, as it's based on who you really are and what you want. Don't commit to things that aren't important to you. You won't stick to them, and they will just provide fodder for your inner critic.

Decide that you are going to do something and stick to it. This is easier when it is something you actually want, based on the work you have done so far in this book.

If you only do one thing today that makes an impact:

Write down five reasons why it is critical for you to reach your goal.

23. Don't quit

Failure is a funny old concept. We know intellectually that failure is necessary, and that it's OK, as long as we pick ourselves up and learn from it. But we are also aware that there is a delta between knowing something and actually believing it.

When we fear failure, we buy into the belief that whatever action we take will be wrong. It is because we have already set a clear expectation of what success looks like, and we are trying to shoe-horn our way into it.

What if we entered into a new task, or one we have failed at before, with the spirit of curiosity, adventure and fun? It would take the pressure off the end result. Instead, the focus shifts to the exploration of the process, the journey. So what if our action doesn't pay off at the end? What we generate then is information that we can use the next time we try. Or we might conclude that this is not something that deserves any further energy from us.

I have news for you – there is no end point called failure. Why? Because once we have tried something and failed at it, it has brought us so much clarity that we cannot help but want to try it again, or course-correct and try something new.

Giving the outcome of your actions a purpose means they can't fail.

I see potential failure as a deduction process. You have to take action in an area to find out whether it is something you are truly passionate about pursuing, or to see if it can be eliminated from your activities.

What I am saying is that any action is good. It doesn't matter if it is 'right' or 'wrong', as long as you are in movement. When you are moving, you can correct your course. It is very challenging to move the wheel of a car if it is stalled. You can move as slowly and cautiously as you like – just *move*.

REAL-LIFE EXAMPLE: FAIL FAST

My first business coach used to say, 'Fail fast'. That scared me then, but I get it now. Why would you drag out a step that you could just get over and done with and be able to move on from? Some five years after I started working with her, she now tells this story to illustrate her point beautifully: In 2019, she set out to fail nineteen times. By the time she had failed the sixth time, she had doubled the size of her company! I have to tell you that her company is not a piddly one-person band, it was turning over $7 million at the time. Do the math, as she would say...

One might say that in 2019, I had two failed business partnerships and one failed marriage. Emotionally, this was a devastating year for me. But it was also the year that brought me the most clarity. I was reminded that making decisions from a place of not feeling good enough doesn't work. I realised that I had a huge amount of freedom to run my business and my life the way I want to. A fear of what would happen to my daughter and her feelings could easily have kept me in a marriage that wasn't working for me anymore. Instead our little family is working better than ever – we just aren't living together anymore.

Fear keeps you still. It keeps you in relationships where you're not at your best, partnerships that are unbalanced, and jobs that bring you no joy or growth. Having a healthy disregard for your fear of failure will move you forward. And opening your arms to potential failure will increase your pace. You only need to do this once to see the evidence of this being true. Failure is necessary to grow, and it is the best strategy to speed that growth up.

I love this quote from *Big Magic* by Elizabeth Gilbert, where she lists all the fears that come with being a writer and the creative process – all the ways that she could have been stopped writing her books before they became bestsellers. After she lists two pages of fears, she says:

> 'Listen, I don't have all day here… I'll just wrap up my summary this way: SCARY, SCARY, SCARY. Everything is so goddamn scary.'

So, if *everything* is scary, you can't let it stop you!

Failure is a junction

Remember, the only reason you would stop reaching for your goals is if you were to believe you'd failed. Keep going until you succeed. Failure is not an end point – it is simply a junction.

Sometimes fear makes it feel like spaghetti junction, but it is a junction all the same. If you go one way and realise it isn't the one that works for you, you can turn back or get off at the next exit. Who knows, maybe there is something on the detour that was meant for you. Maybe you will get an opportunity that you would never have got if you hadn't gone that way. With this perspective, you are guaranteed to get to the top of your game. So, go ahead and fail – the faster the better.

There are so many things that can come from 'failure', we have to stop loading it with so much power over us. I get why you have previously avoided it – it comes from a desire to be good, to get things right. We want to get a 'well done', just like we did as children. But we are teaching people how to treat us, right? So when we are not willing to fail, it tells the people following our lead that they can't fail either.

If you aren't willing to fail, you have to give up on innovation. In this fast-moving digital age, can you really afford to do that?

Let's shift focus and see if this makes a difference. As a seasoned product development professional, my attitude was that I would have to try a number of solutions before I found the one that worked. I didn't expect everything to work straight away. But I wanted one thing to stand out as better than the others eventually.

This is a valuable lesson in perspective. If I didn't find a solution first try, I wouldn't have stopped looking. I would have kept going until I found one.

Think about that for a moment. When you have a goal, when do you stop? If you don't stop until you reach the goal, surely there isn't any way you can fail...

Failure is really a premature ending. How long have scientists been looking for a cure for cancer? They aren't going to stop and say there isn't a solution – they are going to keep going until they find one. And guess what? When they do, they will start looking for an improved one. Be the person who doesn't quit until they find the best solution.

Don't give up

As we talked about with bravery, and as you will have noticed from the structure of this book, all of this advice is based on you first becoming clear on who you are and what you really want, so you know with the utmost confidence that the goals you are aiming for are worthwhile. If you hadn't done this work, then you could be reading this wondering about the risk of flogging a dead horse.

You may be wondering, 'When is the right time to give up?'

My answer is: 'Reframe that.' In my view, you should develop an attitude of never quitting. You may of course readjust the target, but you must never quit.

I have had to readjust in my time, to keep perspective – I still do. Like in my product development example above, if I had written some requirements for a solution in 1995 and hadn't found it by now, I can safely say the world has changed. Technology has moved on, there are now new buyers in the market, and their needs will have shifted. Look up, see what is going on around you, and revisit your goals to see if they are still relevant. Then carry the same level of commitment to achieving them.

When you are committed to keeping going, it can feel tiring. That is why the power of the impact you will make has to be big enough. Think back to the beginning of this book and the clarity you achieved. Now that you have come this far, you can probably envisage an even bigger impact. Picture this in your mind. When you want to give up, when impostor syndrome tries to wheedle its way back in, you can use everything you have learned so far to take a breath and get back on track.

Keeping going doesn't have to be relentless. Imagine if you worked seven days a week full-time (perhaps you do)... it wouldn't be long before you were sick and burnt-out. Your body needs to rest, as does your mind. You need to build in resilience to your approach so you can reset yourself and go on with renewed energy. Be kind to yourself in this process. Empathise with how you're feeling.

If you only do one thing today that makes an impact:

What can you have another go at today? If there is no pressure, try a new approach to it.

24. Empathy

> 'I've learned that people will forget what you said,
> people will forget what you did, but people will
> never forget how you made them feel.'
> — Maya Angelou

Every time I work with a client, there is some work conversation that comes up. It normally comes in the form of a complaint followed by, 'Why don't they get it?'

By the time you are asking this question, you have already set yourself up to fail. You have preloaded your words with assumptions that ensure the person on the receiving end will have no chance of landing on the positive side of the conversation.

When you go into conversations like this, you are looking only for evidence that confirms what you already believe – so you might as well not bother having that conversation at all. This being the case, you have nothing to lose by doing what I am about to recommend.

If you have taken on board everything that I have said so far, the thing that is likely to come flying back to haunt you here is the 'responsibility versus blame' argument. (But they are x, so why should I y?)

Take responsibility *now* for what comes out of your mouth and know that the response you get is directly correlated.

When I go and speak to companies, it seems no matter where I go, someone gives me an example of a conversation and asks if I think they were aggressive or too blunt. If a person is raising this question, they already know the answer. They should see their question as a red flag that they need to change how they show up.

What these questioners are really looking for is something they can do differently so that they don't call their behaviour into question. They want to stop their nagging self-doubt. But they also want to be right! In my experience, their improvement will not involve changing the point they are making, but their delivery of it.

If you start saying 'yes' when you mean 'no' just so you appear less aggressive, that is going to leave you frustrated in the long run. It is important to tell the truth with clarity, but to pump as much kindness into it as possible.

Take eleven seconds longer

If your answer is 'no' and it is unclear, people will keep bothering you with the same questions and you will lose patience. This problem was raised by a lady I met when I gave a talk at a prestigious London company in the summer of 2019. The people she was being blunt towards deduced that she was grumpy, but they didn't get her point. They formed an opinion about her when she spoke to them, because she didn't appear to care about their feelings. Compare these two responses:

1. **Her response:** 'No, we don't have time for new proposals. We've got no budget!'

2. **My version:** 'I really appreciate the time you've taken to put this proposal together, but given the number of competing priorities for budget, we are going to have to park this for now. I'm sorry. It's highly unlikely that we will be able to review any new proposals until next year now, so why don't you hang on to this and perhaps resubmit it then? Thank you.'

Both are a 'no', but one makes me feel like an idiot, while the other is disappointing, but it acknowledges me, explains to me why the answer is 'no', and closes with appreciation.

How much longer did it take? Eleven seconds, I reckon.

It would only take an extra eleven seconds to speak from the heart rather than your disgruntled head. It's worth it, when you consider the cost of leaving a person feeling undervalued, and you going to bed later saying mean things to yourself about your behaviour.

Just be considerate.

If you are talking to people at work like this, chances are, you are speaking to your loved ones in an even worse tone. You will end up alienating people and feeling alone and unsupported. And if you are talking to your loved ones like this, then you are talking to yourself even more critically. What you hear in your head is *your* voice, not what other people are saying.

This is one of the biggest lessons I learned on my own transformational journey. People used to say I was cold because I was decisive. I could have been even more effective if I had infused the communication of my decisions with love and kindness.

People don't come to work wanting to do a poor job. But that is what they will do if they don't feel appreciated. As a leader, it is your role to show people you care, whether they report to you or not. Telling yourself you're too busy or don't have time to do that is a poor assessment of what counts.

When people are curt and decisive, it is normally because they don't want to be challenged, because they are not sure they have a suitable response. People who communicate in this way are in desperate need of approval. They daren't ask open questions, in case you disagree with them. Perhaps this is because they are a little righteous, but what is more likely is that they are struggling with their own inner soundtrack. Being decisive is their attempt to present as strong, good enough, infallible. What that fails to do is effectively cover up that inside, they are feeling like an impostor and are in need of help but have no idea who it is safe to ask without being judged. They also aren't experienced in asking for it. Asking for help is a sign of weakness, they believe.

If I were to summarise what is going on here, it is a lack of self-esteem. I am often asked to explain arrogance, and I say that it is sometimes a complete lack of self-knowledge – refer those people to Sections 1 and 2 of this book. Or it is low self-esteem that is being poorly deflected. When you lack self-esteem, you are highly unlikely to communicate with love because you carry little or none for yourself. You can't give what you don't have, and so when it comes to kindness, it can't be communicated outwardly to others if none exists inside you, for yourself.

When you are ill, do you look after yourself like you would your small child, or do you power on and ignore what your body needs? I used to do this, and it was a fast route to martyrdom. The truth was, I didn't want anyone to know that I could be taken out of the game by something as simple as a cold. But it happens to millions of people every year, so why shouldn't it happen to me?

Disregarding your own well-being doesn't help anyone, and it sets a poor example for the next generation, who you are teaching that it is not OK to look after yourself or be sick. Ignoring this advice will simply raise the level of stress in your organisation.

If you only do one thing today that makes an impact:

Have a conversation today in which you invest an extra eleven seconds, and speak from the heart.

25. Cast a consistent shadow

If I asked you to draw a timeline of your life right now, it would probably look something like a jagged pattern of ups and downs that has had you trying to keep up. This book is about you taking back control, building in more ups, and smoothing the edges off any downs.

We need to have downs as well as ups, otherwise life would be flat. But to reach our ultimate objective of feeling at peace, we want to reduce the range between your peaks and troughs, so that you feel stable and more consistent. You can do this with the inputs you make – intentional actions that are for a clear purpose. The stability you achieve with this will land with others, too.

'Shadow of a Leader' was a concept taught to me aged twenty-four by my late ex-father-in-law. He said:

> 'Your leadership has to be consistent. Your people need to know who you are from one day to the next. Their day can't depend on your mood.'

You can have some oscillation en route to being the best leader you can be, provided you join the dots for people, and it has to be within a tolerable range. You can't be happy one day and moody the next, wanting to joke around one day and be stern and serious the next. People have to understand who you are and how you show up, consistently.

This is something I have found challenging, as I can come across in this way. I take things seriously, but I like to have fun. It seemed, early in my career, that I had to choose one or the other, and I struggled with that. Just because I'm laughing, it doesn't mean that I am not giving the task in hand 100% focus. If you have ever seen me speak live, I am high in energy, yet all the pictures of me show me with a stern expression. I want my messages to land, I want to make an impact on my audience, and I look serious when I do that. At the same time, I manage what might have previously felt laborious or painful with humour, once the audience has my trust. It puts people at ease. Somehow, now, I can blend two seemingly different sides of my personality. What changed?

I allowed myself to be all of who I am.

I stopped worrying about whether people would like me or not and had a healthy disregard for people who delivered criticism. I also established some boundaries when it came to receiving it. Anyone is welcome to give me feedback, but I will only accept it if they give me the opportunity to welcome it, and if it is delivered with genuinely good intention.

Do all the things I have said in this book and you, too, can reveal the very best of you, even if it has been previously criticised. Sometimes you might hear feedback that hurts, but you will have the awareness to know when they have a fair point, and it might be something you want to work on. It won't mean you have to lock down part of your personality, or start being someone you are not. It may mean you have compromised on one of your values. When I am off my game, or have been acting in a way I am not proud of, it is usually because my kindness meter is down. I focus on kindness and find a way to clean up what I have done. This is my ongoing pattern of awareness and bravery.

None of this is about being perfect. It is about being consistent enough that you know when something needs to be addressed in your leadership, and you are courageous enough to do it. The quicker you address, it the less like bravery it feels. People think I am incredibly brave, but in fact bravery is built into who I am now. I have practised it and become consistent with it, even when my brain wants to talk me out of it. My focus is on clean energy. I don't want to carry guilt from conversation to conversation or decision to decision. I want to be able to sleep easily at night.

Showing up consistently is the ultimate example to set the people following your lead, whether they work for you or not. It means they will always know where they stand with you, and it will make it easy for them to come to you with new ideas, ask you for help, or tell you when they are not sure they can deliver on time after all. Things that would previously have sent you and, therefore, them into a tailspin, will no longer be an issue, because you'll have ditched all the unhealthy patterns that weren't serving you – like judgement, perfectionism and fear of failure. Your new perspective and your ability to reframe quickly will become embedded in your character, and people will be inspired by it. Imagine the positive ripples you'll create in the organisation of the future with this outlook and modus operandi.

My ex-husband is a classic example of the value clarity brings. When he enters a venue where he coaches tennis, children run to him and hug him. From this, I deduced that he must be a real softie on the court. But when I first saw him coaching them, I was surprised – he is strict and sometimes curt. Above all, though, he is clear. He is consistent. They have absolute faith in his instruction and know that he will keep them safe. As long as they stay within the rules and boundaries he has set, he is great for them to be around.

When you think of other leaders at work, who are the people that you don't hesitate to approach? Even if it's someone who is consistently miserable, you can predict their behaviour, and know what they will be like from one day to the next.

What I regularly hear on the flip side, though, is that when the meetings that need to be arranged, requests made, and approvals granted involve someone inconsistent, this is where the problems lie.

People need to know that they can come and ask you questions, that they can share when they reach a failure junction without you blowing a gasket. It doesn't matter if you are not the best you can be yet. Start by being consistent. Consistency brings steadiness. And knowing you are safe in this way will meet your team's most basic level of human need.

Being consistent means that the people around you can grow in confidence. The more stability they experience, the braver they will be, and the less affected you will all be by external factors outside your control, like other people and the market environment.

If you only do one thing today that makes an impact:

Be consistent all day, regardless of your mood.

Making It Count

Now is when you will start to see the fruits of your labour. I think you'll agree that the relative effort so far has been low, but the results are about to start coming in.

26. Your contribution

I meet a lot of women who refer to time running out. They aren't talking about their biological clock – they are talking about their career. People as young as twenty-eight have told me that they have this fear, but it is the women aged thirty-nine and over who are more acutely aware that the time to play bigger is *now*. And they are right.

While I believe that it is never too late to change course in the direction of what you really want, I also believe that there is no time like the present. Allowing yourself to stagnate is a sure way to make your transformation more difficult and fuel your inner critic.

I know it may feel like having a lot of experience boxes you in, but it isn't true. The only thing boxing you in is the lens through which you are viewing your future. Whatever your age, taking the opportunity to look at what you have to offer is always a surprising, liberating and empowering experience. I have to say, it is easier when people remind you of what you have done... but of course, you can take responsibility and remind yourself.

If I asked you to look back on the last year and tell me the best bits that happened, you would likely struggle. Why? Because it feels like an age away, and despite our best efforts, the things that didn't go so well are likely to be at the forefront of our minds, rather than all the small wins, which may have gone uncelebrated.

EXERCISE: THE JOLLY JAR

I came up with the idea to create a 'Jolly Jar' some years ago, and now many women are doing this, both in leadership at work and by setting a great example for their children at home.

Jolly Jars are made in primary schools for the Christmas tombola – old jars are cleaned and decorated, then filled with sweets or little toys. A simple concept that brings a lot of joy. I wanted to use the concept to bring *myself* joy. It came to me at a time when I felt rejection more than I felt success. I wanted to draw on my joy from the other fifty weeks of the year, when the jar was redundant. So I came up with this exercise.

Every Friday, I write on a small piece of paper the best thing that I *made* happen that week. If at any time I feel low, I take a piece of paper out of the jar and remind myself how valuable my contribution is. I can also measure how far I have come – that piece of paper might have been from three or six months earlier. If you are making a contribution towards your goal every single day, and the jar contains the highlight from that week, you'll soon notice how significantly you're moving on over the course of a year.

The Jolly Jar focuses on all your positives, by its nature, but when you are looking at the contribution you have made over the course of your life or career, there will be gold in the negative stuff as well. This perspective ensures we don't ever feel that time has been wasted.

If I look at my own career, for example, being bullied in my last contract role in the NHS was possibly the best thing that could have happened to me. Though it was horrific at the time, it was the jolt I needed to start my full-time coaching business. I would prefer that over a health scare any day of the week.

Life kicks us up the backside sometimes. What I want for you is to not hang around waiting for that to happen to you. I pushed myself for years, not being kind enough to give myself a moment's rest. But when I got sick in 2009, I had to stop. On the night before my first day working for the NHS, I felt seriously unwell. I had a pain in my back that was so bad, I couldn't lie down, and was finding it hard to breathe. The doctor dismissed it as indigestion, despite me having been sleeping upright for ten days. Finally, I went to A and E only to discover that I had pulmonary embolisms on both lungs. I was very nearly dead.

I could use this story to illustrate a number of things. When the doctor came back to me with the news, he was apologetic: 'I'm sorry, you really didn't look this sick.'

My brave face had nearly killed me.

I learned a lot from that time. Life is short. Like actually, properly short, not just throwaway-comment short. This was a stark reminder to slow down, appreciate what's going on right now and stop rushing myself to a meaningless goal. I started to listen to my body, and made a decision to make every moment count towards my own happiness and fulfilment.

Allow this to be your kick up the backside. Don't wait to get ill, to lose a relationship or to create circumstances that cause you shame. Take ownership of your life now and decide how you are going to make it count. Live a life of significance and intention, and don't discount what you have generated so far.

Review the positives – and the negatives

If everything absolutely *had* to happen the way it has done up until this point, what evidence has it created that will serve your future? Be proactive and start to look at what has made the biggest contribution. Look at the positives:

- The opportunities

- The praise you have been given

- The awards you have won

- The bonuses you have been paid

- The touching notes in your Christmas cards from employees

And the negatives:

- All the jobs you didn't get

- The people who dumped you

- The terrible holiday

- The friend who ghosted you

- The house that fell through

My perspective on negatives is that they happened for a reason. Not just that, they needed to happen to change my course. I see them, therefore, as bullets dodged. If you put 'Thank goodness for' in front of all of those negative items, you will be able to see the light that they brought in. For me, it is almost always that they saved me time. Time is extremely precious to me, and the thought of wasting it turns my stomach. When a friend ghosted me, it was painful, but when I look back on it, she was always letting me down at the last minute – clearly she didn't want to be my friend anymore, so the end of the friendship allowed me to stop putting energy into it and move on.

When I look at the successes I have in my business, I can normally trace them back to a negative, which created the space for a new, brave request that culminated in a 'yes'. One yes always generates more opportunities, but you have to have space for them first.

Mine your experience for all the things that have been negative, then identify the positive that happened soon afterwards. Doing this will not only help you reframe your past, but it will also mean that you get excited when you face a perceived failure or rejection – it means something bigger and better is coming!

If you have experienced a recent negative, give it time. You don't need to put pressure on yourself to rush your emotional healing or find the lesson. When you are in pain, you can't get this perspective. Do this exercise for times you have healed already and practise linking them to the opportunity that followed.

When the opportunity shows up for your more recent experience, you will then see it more quickly.

This dot-joining experience is missing from so many professional women's lives. They move around at such a pace that they are in constant overwhelm. If you have not put into practice what I said about focus, and you have not set your sights on areas of impact that match who you are, you won't feel like you are making progress. If you have done those things and you still don't feel like you are making progress, then it is because you are moving from one activity to another too quickly to allow time to collect positive evidence.

Slow down, look at where you have been spending your time, and select the bits that count for your Jolly Jar. This is your jar of evidence. This is your source of self-belief when you feel lacking. This is your reminder of how brilliant you are, and why you must keep going. This is your process for making sure you never have to wrack your brains for why you're an amazing leader. This is what is going on your CV from now on. These are the things you mention when you meet people. Do you see?

If you only do one thing today that makes an impact:

Pick a negative experience and identify one positive thing that could only have happened as a result of it.

27. You are the product

For many years, I was an award-winning marketer in global telecoms, and, truth be told, I was a rock star in the realm of product development. When I think about why that was, it was because I was highly commercial, and I delivered the products and projects that I said I would. In other words, I could be trusted to have clear purpose and commitment to keep going until the end.

I was clear about what the product did and didn't do, who it was for, and why the customer would buy it. It resulted in masses of sales and long-term contracts based on the vision I had painted for the product roadmap.

Today, you are my product. You might not have drawn the analogy yet with what I just said, but marketing yourself is no different from marketing anything else. A winning product has to be highly relevant and aligned with the target market's needs and desires. If you can be the answer to someone else's perceived problem, then *you* are winning.

There are people who need your skills, abilities and personality right now. But there are two problems:

1. You don't know who your customer is and what they need

2. The customer isn't aware of their needs either

The chances of you matching these up are impossible.

The job that is perfect for you doesn't exist yet, because you haven't created an awareness of the need yet.

When I say this to my clients, their minds are blown. Then they realise the power of what I said. The jobs that you are looking at online and considering applying for right now are way too comfortable for you. They have been lived in before, expectations have been set about how they might be done, and there is a concept of what good performance in that role looks like already. But the one that matches everything you have to offer can only be done by you. There is no competition for the job that you will do and love at some point in the near future. It's up to you to create the vision for your future, and your roadmap to it.

Fast-track your route to your dream job

We all know what we would love to do, or have never done, but are interested in. What is the role you would love to do? The sooner you are clear on what it is that you want to do at work, and where you want to spend your time, the better. Maybe you are interested in artificial intelligence or machine learning to get more women to the top of organisations. (I think women are harder to replace than men!)

Whatever it is, write a list of all the things you are excited about. What are all the things you would love to work on next, or in the future?

I am going to show you how to fast-track your positioning for this using LinkedIn, in five easy steps.

Step 1: What in your experience so far contributes?

Have a look at your LinkedIn profile and compare it with your wish list. Chances are, it mirrors your CV and shows all the things you were responsible for or have delivered in the past. But remember, what got you here won't get you to the new place that you have envisaged. Reframe all the things you have written on your CV so people can see how they lay the ground for the vision you have created. Delete stuff that doesn't contribute – that means things you didn't enjoy, things that have no relevance to the job you want to do. You don't want to be hired for something you never want to do again.

Step 2: Market yourself so you are the obvious choice

You have cleaned up the past to fit your vision for the future. Now you have to focus on your present contribution. Communicate where you are now by making sure your daily activity on LinkedIn aligns with your goals.

Rob McCargow is a great example of this – once an executive recruiter, he is now a leading voice on AI, and there is rarely a tech or AI conference that he doesn't speak at. This is because he mined his experience for what made the greatest impact – networking, communication and commercial awareness – and he used these to remarket himself. It took time for Rob to find his purpose and decide what he was going to become well known for. It is possible, though, to go from no one to expert in as little as six weeks on LinkedIn. I achieved that as a telepresence managed service specialist long before LinkedIn was even a thing, purely because of focus. How? Because I talked about nothing else. I was prolific, so people would put me and telepresence together in most sentences. That's what you are doing here – becoming the obvious choice from your focus on one thing.

Step 3: Create content that fits your vision

Create articles on your thoughts about your single vision. If you are stuck, writing a discussion piece is a great approach. Raise a question in the title that you are interested in, and share your views, experience and questions on it. Inviting comment will attract all the people with an opinion in your area whose posts you can then focus on.

Step 4: Get your endorsements up to date

Define the top ten skills that fit the role you want and ask five people a week to endorse you for them. Delete all the other ones that conflict. I had to do this when I wanted to shift from being a product specialist to a leadership one. People still endorse me for my product skills, but this chapter will show you how I have spun that to be relevant to leadership and positioning people for top jobs. What is coaching, really? It is helping people to match themselves to the environment they want. That's just top-class marketing as far as I am concerned! See how I have mined my past to make it relevant to my future? Not only that – it makes me trusted as a coach who has the ability to do that well.

Step 5: Ask for recommendations

As you do more and more relevant work, and you get recognition for it, ask people *in real time* to send you a recommendation. Don't give them a week to do it, because they will forget. Ask them if they have five minutes to do it now. It is important to get energetic words into your profile so that when recruiters and people in your organisation are looking (because believe me, they are), you stand out for all the right reasons. Social proof is more powerful than anything else when it comes to getting introductions into new areas. If you make clear what you care about, what you'd love to learn and where you want to be next, people will hire you because you stand out – they can teach you the knowledge that you don't have yet. Remember, it only took me six weeks to be *the* expert in telepresence. That's only the equivalent of the school summer holidays.

I can't wait to see your thought leadership on Linked-In! Connect with me at www.linkedin.com/in/susie-ramroop-mindset-coach – oh, and take five minutes to write me a LinkedIn recommendation, would you? Thanks.

If you only do one thing today that makes an impact:

Go to your LinkedIn profile and delete five things from the last two years of your CV that you would never want to do again.

28. Launching the new you

In the same way that you have created a story on LinkedIn that makes you the natural choice for the things you have set your sights on, your conversations now need to reflect the same patterns.

When you meet people for the first time, you are marketing yourself to them. Whatever you tell them is how they will remember you – so make it count. When I met Louise, she told me about all the things she does in her life. To me, she sounded like an overwhelmed mum. When she networked with people, she told them about her current job. Luckily for her, she came on one of my retreats and we were able to get clear on what it is she really wants when she is not pleasing other people and trying to maintain her popularity. (Sorry, Lou!) While all of that made her feel good, she was bored and uninspired at work, yet highly capable, and enjoying the organisation she worked for.

Louise has a way of engaging and communicating with people that was frankly being wasted in her role. She wasn't leveraging that at all. As I got to know her over the three-day retreat, she showed me professional passions that she never talked about, deep knowledge about all sorts of areas about life, and she revealed to me what a strategic thinker she was. She wasn't using any of that in her role as a Project Manager.

Louise was doing that classic thing of waiting to be offered a role, any role, and then being so flattered that she would take it. She was not in the driving seat of her career.

Like Louise, you have a whole host of talents that you are sitting on and not valuing. Why? Because the role you are in is too small for you. Let me explain. Until now, you have been in survival mode worrying about how to do a good enough job and wondering whether anyone is noticing you – you are not showing up to work as your best self that way. Instead, the energy that you bring to work must be focused on your clear future, and your focus for each day in your current role must be on exercising your muscles for the role in that future. Consciously making this your practice gives you purpose and intention. It doesn't matter that your current role isn't an exact fit. Make the most of it. Leverage this time.

Maybe you don't like your current role. Even more reason why you need to make it work for you. You are in your role for a reason – it is so you can build a track record of creating contribution wherever you go. It's like media training – you are taught how to make the point you want to make regardless of the question you are asked. It is real time reframing in a seamless and elegant way.

Have the conversation you want to have

Make sure your vision for the future is present in every conversation you have. When you network with people, introduce your vision and tell them where you are on the path towards it. For example:

> THEM: What do you do, Susie?
> ME: I'm writing my first business book at the moment and looking for opportunities to speak to promote it.

The person asking 'What do you do?' was not looking for that answer. They were making conversation and hoping to goodness that the person on the end of the question had something to say that might actually interest them. Thankfully, I did.

Compare my answer with muttering something about your current job and transferring all of the negativity and insecurity you feel about it to them. Which one is going to leave them feeling inspired and desperate to talk about you to the people in their network? They are looking for the parallels between you and them. If there isn't one, they will start searching their mind for someone they know who aligns with what you just said.

Introducing myself based on my vision is going to get the other person thinking about who they know who can help me, or at least buy the book.

Raise the bar and make it useful. We teach people how to treat us, remember?

Teach people who you are going to be so that they can be enrolled in helping you get there. If I had met Louise only the first time, I might have thought of her if ever I saw a telecoms project manager job come up. Now that she has elevated her vision, I am looking out for Director of Strategy roles in organisations with strong values and a current or desired digital roadmap. She has given me a clear vision of where her next step is, so now I am focused on her goal, not her role. Try this with all the people you meet and see how quickly the perfect opportunity comes to you.

Think about it. When you meet people, how many times do you describe your current role with excitement and pride? Think about what you are conveying to people. What action would they take on your behalf now that they have met you, based on how you showed up?

When I speak at events, people talk about it for weeks afterwards on LinkedIn. Why? Because I share valuable insights in a way that reflects my personality – people feel like they have got to know me and they know what I stand for. I tell personal stories that show how far I have come – I want people to think, 'Well if she can, I can too.'

Join the dots for people

I didn't become a speaker or an author overnight. I had plenty of years where I went through all the things in chapter one. And two, and three. You are not the only one. But knowing that is not enough. You need to reflect on and activate new thinking based on all the sections of this book. I appreciate that not everyone is built in a way that they can take the information from a book and totally transform their life. That's OK. But if you *are* one of them, don't sit there with that and move on to the next one in your reading pile. This book is it. It is enough. You could amplify your experience by gifting a copy of this book to a friend and going on this journey together. If there isn't anyone in your immediate network who can help with this, feel free to get in touch with me and see if I can help. I mean it. I have found most of my coaches through reading their book first. If we hit it off, it could mean you are a success story in my next book!

Mentioning your internal network might have just taken the wind out of your sails. If it did, notice that. Plenty of people have said that you are the product of the five people you spend the most time with. If those people are your family members who, no matter what you do, only see you as a child, are your ex-colleagues who compete with you, or your friend who talks about themselves the whole time, then you may need to review who's on your team.

You need people around you who are going to buy into your vision or who love you enough to stand by you until they understand it. It was clear to me when I started my own coaching business that I didn't have anyone in my network who was an entrepreneur, a professional speaker, or a leader in their industry. I didn't really have anyone to look up to – I *was* that person for most of my network. My mum's energy around my business and my struggle for the first three years was fearful. Many of my friends didn't like the fact that I was having a different level of conversation now that involved going way beyond entertaining them, and so it left me feeling lonely, uninspired and unsupported.

When people have known you for a while, and they can see the path you have trodden, plotting a new one and embarking on a new way of operating might feel confusing to them. And, putting it bluntly, they might not want to join you on it. I have lost several friends on my journey to where I am now, and for whatever reason, they have removed themselves from my life. I didn't do anything other than become more of who I already am, and reveal who I am destined to be, but the most surprising relationships can be affected by this. Equally, it might become obvious to you, once you are clear of your new direction, that the people in your life are not making a positive contribution. At this point you have a choice – either bring them with you or let them go. When you have been friends with people for a long time, this can generate a lot of fear, but if those emotions are coming up, acknowledge them. I was sad when some of my relationships ended, but I reframed that. It was clearly best for both of us that we spend time with people who are compatible with how we want to live our lives.

Choose your network

I had to consciously choose better people to be around. People who could comprehend and support where I was headed, and who wouldn't try and talk me out of what I wanted. When you are in the workplace, there are going to be some people who are better to be around than others. By showing up as you, by asking great questions that show a genuine interest in people, you are going to stand out as being different. You are not trying to fit what exists – you are setting a new tone to which all the right people will gravitate.

If you are in meetings that you previously deemed boring, don't lower yourself to that energy, bring new energy and ask great questions that encourage people to break free from the patterns that don't serve them. You don't need to call them out as such. Just call into question their black and white statements. Those people who say, 'always' and 'never' with some negative connotation, just need you to hold up the mirror with a simple, 'Really? Always?' It can be done with a big smile and a lot of love. One great question has the power to disrupt the status quo and re-energise within seconds.

Networking in this modern age is about making connections. Those connections, if they are going to work for you personally and professionally, have to be based on who you really are. They have to be able to see you before they can help and support you. Surface level conversation won't cut it. Yes, you need to paint a vision, but they also want to see heartfelt reasons about why it is important to you.

Being vulnerable doesn't have to mean baring your soul to the next person you meet, but it means being prepared to ask real questions and share your feelings rather than just your thoughts.

Like your LinkedIn profile, you can choose what exists in your conversations. You don't have to tell your backstory or share things you're not proud of or happy about. Focus on what you want and provide the content that supports your vision. That way, any true feelings of vulnerability can relate to the things you haven't experienced yet. And then when people look you up on LinkedIn, they see coherence with the person they just met, instead of a list of boring deliverables and responsibilities.

To find great people, you may have to come across the not-so-great. People who decide they don't like you fit in the latter category. They won't be on your team. They won't support you. And they won't ever buy your 'product'. So what? All of this makes them highly irrelevant to you. They have no influence over you. Be true to who you are. You will still have a positive influence on them, whether they like you or not.

People are always watching. Your post might only have two likes, from your friends, but people saw it. It has the power to move them. It is a source of leadership. Let them see you.

If you only do one thing today that makes an impact:

Write yourself a two-line introduction of how you will introduce yourself in two years, when you have reached your goal. Then go to a networking event and use it there with active intention.

29. Stop trying to be the expert

No one lays out for you how to get from management to leadership. We go from doing all the things that make us good at our jobs, to doing a management course that helps us with all the boring HR mechanics (sorry, but they are indeed dull), and no one tells us how to engage with people to get the best from them. Actually, what this does is put the spotlight on us and how we work. Leadership is not about you – it is about the people around you and the impact you have on them.

Poor leadership creates emotions in other people that can be damaging. How you show up as a leader sets the tone for everyone around you. We've all seen it – in the boss who stays late in the office, so makes it challenging for you to leave on time. I had a boss that had a penchant for producing reams and reams of documents, so she created a standard for everyone else, even though more often than not this wasn't their strength.

Take a moment to define the sort of leader you want to be. Your definition could well be based on all the leaders you have vowed never to be like throughout your career to date.

What is great leadership to you? For me, great leadership is not about knowing more than everyone else. Great leadership is about unlocking talent and nurturing it such that everyone can grow.

It is an error, in my view, to promote someone to a leadership position because they know the most or have been there the longest. I have had countless people work for me who were very senior, and even paid as much as I was, but I would never have put them in a leadership role, and nor did they want one.

Being the most knowledgeable doesn't make you the best leader. Leadership requires a fondness of and an interest in people. To unlock the best in them, they need to know you care. In my experience, I've seen many leaders who don't enjoy the people part, yet they are heads of and directors of the business. If they are honest, what motivated them to get there is their ego in terms of the status and the pay packet. But in fairness to them, it is also because when you are good at your job and at the top of your pay grade, a promotion is often perceived to be the next logical step.

This pattern of promoting the most knowledgeable, particularly in fields like STEM (science, technology, engineering and maths), mean that you often get people in leadership positions feeling like they need to know as much as the technical teams to feel good enough.

Conversely, I believe I could go into any organisation and lead them effectively. How can that be? Because I don't need to know the answers, I just need to know how to get them from the people in the teams. I need to know how to unlock their creativity. The way to do this is through asking great questions, not by having all the answers.

Ask, don't tell

For years, I have been coaching leaders who are frustrated with their teams because they aren't working in the way that they want. They tend to resort to telling them at this point, and then get even more frustrated when it isn't done exactly to the letter. This dictatorial approach doesn't work. It makes people on the receiving end feel unvalued, stifles their creativity, and it completely tramples on their confidence.

Even if you are the most knowledgeable, when you shift to the role of leader, it is not about proving your individual worth, it is about collectively gathering the value of the whole team.

Many clients of mine have expressed a fear that if they ask their teams a question, it will open the floodgates and nothing will get done. This isn't true – your questions don't have to be global ones that invite lots of irrelevant noise, they can be tight and targeted. Teach people to be succinct and focused on the solution.

Here are some great questions you can ask your team:

- If we had six weeks to do this, what would be step one on your plan?

- What is the one thing that is in the way of x?

- What is one thing we could get done if we had all the time in the world?

- If we were 10% more creative, what feature could we add to these requirements?

- What is the best example of an intranet in our organisation?

- If we pumped a bit more compassion into that, what do we think the real reason is behind x?

- If you had to state the problem in two sentences, what is it?

- If you had to pay for this out of your own pocket, what solution would you choose?

- What single element of that could you get delivered this week?

- What do you need me to take off your plate for you to get this thing done?

- What does 'finished' look like for you?

- How will you know when you are at the halfway point? Why don't we schedule a catch up on Wednesday to review [the detail of how they just described the halfway point]?

- When you take this to the board, what do you predict will be the reason they reject it?

- Can I ask a basic question?

- Forgive me, can we take a breath and look at this through a really simple lens that I can easily understand...

Help people to get clarity. Change their pace. Focus them on isolating an area of improvement, so they can target their own actions. Get them to start by being 1% braver, more creative, more compassionate. When they are clear, it is so much easier for them to get excited to deliver. Not only that, but they will own the results.

The problem with being the expert is that we often have a fixed idea about what the outcome will look like. This clear vision typically only exists in our heads, so when we are asking other people to deliver, it is sensible to have them describe to you what it will look like when finished, rather than berate them at the end for not having read your mind and produced your imaginary outcome.

Rise above the detail, lift your gaze, and take people with you. Meet them where they are and help them see what you are looking at. When you are looking at the same thing, then you can have a conversation about how to move forward. Step out of your world first – and meet them in theirs.

When you are the expert, it is tempting to do things yourself or dictate how things ought to be done. But what's the pay-off? This disempowers the people who work for you, and it adds tonnes of pressure on you.

Why be so audacious to believe that you know best? Letting go of this assumption and using your knowledge to stimulate others is so much more powerful.

Don't hold yourself back because you think you don't know enough. The more you know, the more you are trapped in your existing thinking. Asking great questions not only unlocks the talent in front of you, but it unlocks yours, too. It allows you to learn new things, get excited about your work, and be surprised by the results. When you have seen it all before and are closed in your communications, it makes for a boring career, and an unhappy team.

Unlock the brilliance in others. Reveal your own. Do it with great questions.

For more helpful resources, visit www.susieramroop. com.

If you only do one thing today that makes an impact:

Say, 'I don't know', when you really do. And then ask, 'What do you think?' See what you learn...

30. Ask for what you want

As women, we spend a lot of time talking about not getting what we want or rationalising why we won't get or haven't got it. The reason for this, more often than not, is that we haven't actually asked for it.

This came to my awareness when my daughter was about four years old. As I was watching something on TV, she would come in and complain, 'Ohhhhhhhhh, I wanted to watch *myyyy* programme!' It brought with it this heavy weight that is the same one I feel when I am around anyone who complains all the time. Given that I can't choose to avoid her, I thought I'd better find a solution!

When you want something and you lack clarity, it can sound like a statement at best, or a complaint at worst. This is not unique to children, I am just using my pre-schooler to demonstrate that placing your request doesn't require experience, just clarity. I suggested to my daughter that she might get a better response if she tried asking for what she wanted. There was born a new habit. A new mindset. As soon as she sensed something she didn't want, she missed out the complaint and went straight to the request.

Assume you'll get it

I'll be honest, there was still a little moany residue left over. It took me a while to spot, but I realised that asking in itself wasn't enough. My daughter was still asking with a certain tone – one which communicated an expectation that I was going to say 'no'. So, I ramped up my advice to: 'Ask for what you want, and assume you will get it.'

Having a positive expectation for the request changed the dynamic completely. Now I didn't feel that the question was loaded with guilt, I felt that it was one I could consider and answer 'yes' or 'no' to. More often than not, I said 'yes'.

No attachment

This made her happy, but over time I realised that she now coupled asking for what she wanted and assuming she'd get it with getting it all the time. Clearly, this doesn't reflect real life, or match up with my desire to watch *Grey's Anatomy* when I want to, so I decided to amplify it even more:

'Ask for what you want, and assume you will get it, with no attachment to the answer.'

On the occasions I said 'no', she gradually learned to accept that sometimes her request might be refused. Initially, that changed her expectation tone, but over time, she saw that more often than not, I didn't say 'no'.

When I did say 'no', it was carefully delivered, and normally worked in her favour – 'I'm going to watch up until the next ad break and then we can put your programme on, but I need you to let me watch this in peace until then. Deal?'

She was four, remember. Whether you have kids or not, this is a valuable lesson.

We have in our heads that our requests will never be accepted, but it isn't true. Most people are reasonable – you have to give them the best chance of giving you what you want. But if you don't ask, you are cutting off all possibilities.

Don't ask for a pay rise without the full belief that you might get it. It will sound like a complaint, otherwise. Don't muddy your requests with justifications of why you want it. That will also sound like a complaint. And above all, don't use up valuable energy requesting things you don't actually want.

When you shift your focus to asking for what you want and assuming that you will get it, without attachment, you will not only find it easy to ask, but you won't be so caught up in the fear of what people will say when they reject your request. This builds resilience, and it means you can move on – either to your next request, the next person, or to a modification in what you asked for, until it is so irresistible that people can't help but say '*Yes!*'

My daughter, now aged eight, came up with an illuminating point this week. She said, 'Even when you say "no", Mama, it still works out well for me.'

'How so?' I asked.

'When you say "no", I know you are storing up ideas for the future, so if you say "no" now, I know that it gives you ideas for special occasions and presents.'

That child is a genius. Yes!

We teach people how to treat us. Asking for what we want is going to raise the bar for our lives. It is like leaving a breadcrumb trail for people to follow. If you want to speak at a conference, ask. The answer might be 'no' this year, but consider that you are warming them up for next year. If you want to work on a juicy project at work, you are getting on the radar so you are front-of-mind for next time.

People start sentences all the time with, 'How did you get...?' My answer begins the same way every time.

I asked. I ask so much now that I forget what I have asked for half the time. I am so detached from the answer being 'no' that I trust I will be made aware when it is 'yes'.

The more you flex your asking muscle, the more you get. If you use it in the direction towards your one goal, how long do you think it will take to get there compared to the approach you were using before? Not very long.

You won't be looking at other people wondering how they got it. You won't be talking yourself out of it, you will be communicating intentional requests that come from the heart.

You have to invest your energy in what is going to make the difference. I know that by showing up this way, I am inspiring people, and I know you will, too.

I appreciate that this probably makes perfect sense to you, but you haven't necessarily worked out where to start. Let me help. Start at the end of the formula – without attachment. Exercise your asking muscle on things you don't care that much about or believe firmly you won't get at first. I started with things like asking to pay with my store rewards card in fancy restaurants. Or asking whether single people get a free coffee on Valentine's day in Costa. This reflects my humour, and always results in a smile and great banter. It sometimes results in free cake, a £5k pay rise, or massive speaking opportunities.

Remember, none of this is about being perfect. It's about being playful, curious, exploratory, and allowing yourself to reveal who you are in the process.

If you only do one thing today that makes an impact:

Ask for something that isn't available, with the absolute assumption that you might get it.

Conclusion

Well done – you have come a long way. The good news is, your journey never needs to end. The more you follow the model of awareness and bravery in the direction of contribution, the more gold you'll find.

There will come a time when that role you have created in your vision becomes available to you. By then, you will be perfectly positioned, having been flexing all the right muscles this whole time, while having the time of your life. This is what you have been preparing for, the chance to lead in a role that you love, being clear about the impact you can make on the world. This is a job that doesn't feel like work. No effort is required to be the best version of you, just the right context.

You have set up your work environment with a horde of people who have followed your lead, used you as an exemplar, and unlocked their potential. This leaves you with a number of successors to choose from, and no one in a pigeonhole.

Your home life is set up to fuel you and replenish you. There are no compromises required.

Use this book like a guidebook. Use it to deepen your awareness of who you are and what you want. Use it to inspire you to be brave in a way that is barely noticeable to other people. And, above all, use it to make a bigger contribution in the world.

Be the leader that you and all those other people who are sitting where you have been can see: a shining example of what it takes to go first. Be the leader for all those schoolchildren who are being shown brilliant examples of leadership but thinking that it is difficult to achieve. Show up for all those people who have had their confidence knocked and are tempted to play small now. Be the leader you, your family and all the people who have been proud of you all along know you truly are. Believe them now when they tell you how you inspire them.

Have a true sense of urgency about what you have learned in this book, using John Kotter's definition:

> 'Action on critical issues is needed *now*,
> not eventually, not when it fits easily into a
> schedule. *Now* means making real progress
> every single day.'

There is no time to lose. Start *now*.

This is the true essence of making a contribution – to your own life and the lives of all those people looking to you as the leader they want to see.

You are amazing, and I can't wait to see you when you show up to play a bigger game. To make sure I notice, connect with me now on LinkedIn at www.linkedin.com/in/susie-ramroop-mindset-coach, and perhaps share with me your one focus of who you are going to *be* from now on.

Wishing you all the very best,
Susie

Resources

To watch Galia's coaching session on how to generate nervous excitement, visit: www.susieramroop.com/coachingsession

Clear, J (2018) *Atomic Habits*, Random House Business

Covey, SR (1992) *The Seven Habits of Highly Effective People*, Simon and Schuster

De Botton, Alain (2005) *Status Anxiety*, Penguin

Dyer, W (2011) Facebook post

Gallo, C (2014) 'The Maya Angelou Quote that Will Radically Improve Your Business', www.forbes.com/sites/carminegallo/2014/05/31/the-maya-angelou-quote-that-will-radically-improve-your-business/#212dfd57118b

Gilbert, E (2016) *Big Magic: Creative living beyond fear*, Bloomsbury

Goldsmith, M (2010) *What Got You Here Won't Get You There: How successful people become even more successful*, Profile Books

Hay, L (1984) *You Can Heal Your Life*, Hay House

'Johnny Wilkinson, CBE: JLA Speakers Breakfast (2017) www.jla.co.uk/conference-speakers/jonny-wilkinson

Keller, G, and Papasan, J (2014) *The One Thing: The surprisingly simple truth behind extraordinary results*, John Murray Learning

Kessel, A (2016) *Eat Sweat Play: How sport can change our lives*, Macmillan

Kotter, JP (2008) *A Sense of Urgency*, Harvard Business Review

'Lewis Hamilton: "I'm building a masterpiece"' [video] (4 November 2019) www.formula1.com/en/video/2019/11/Lewis_Hamilton___I%27m_building_a_masterpiece__.html

Madam Secretary [television programme] (2019) CBS

McKinsey & Co (2009), *Achieving World Class Productivity in the NHS 2009/10–2013/14: Detailing the size of the opportunity*, Department of Health, www.nhshistory.net/mckinsey%20report.pdf

Norris, B (2020) Author of *The Girl Who Climbed Everest: Lessons learned facing up to the world's toughest mountains*, speaking at a CIO+1 event

Palacio, RJ (2013) *Wonder*, Corgi

Pelicci, Dr G (2016) 'Taking a Leap' Telesummit, available from www.susieramroop.com

Sartre, J-P (2000) *Huis Clos and other Plays: 'The Respectable Prostitute'; 'Lucifer and the Lord'; 'Huis Clos' (translated as 'Hell is Other People')*, Penguin Classics

Soosalu, G, and Oka, M (2012) *mBraining: Using your multiple brains to do cool stuff*, CreateSpace Independent Publishing Platform

Stoltz, PG (2014) *Grit: The new science of what it takes to persevere, flourish, succeed*, Climb Strong Press

Sumpter, S (January 2017) Personal communication at PACE Mastermind

Syed, M (2016) *Black Box Thinking: Marginal gains and the secrets of high performance*, John Murray

Wintle, W (1900) 'Thinking'

Acknowledgements

Like the Oscar speech that everyone just wants to be over...

Thank you, Elise, for all the times you got up but didn't disturb my early morning writing session, when you let me type without interruption and when you found me a pen when I had a burning idea! I don't think I could have done this without your patience and your support. Thank you for your pride and your faith in me.

To Mum and Dad, for your endless support and for not worrying about me this one time when I had a goal no one could quite wrap their head around! Thank you for bolstering me with love when I needed it, for your encouragement to keep going when times got tough and for your constant offers to give me money! I know I have confused you over the years. I hope now you can get a proper glimpse into what I do for a living… I am here because of you, and I thank you from the bottom of my heart for everything you have ever been for me.

Thank you to Omar, for connecting me to my roots, for all the happy times and for making me better. You are a wonderful Papa and I appreciate you for always being willing to team up with Mum and Dad to look after Elise when I run my retreats in the forest. Thank you, too, for those times when I just needed a retreat for myself despite the disruption I know it causes. You will always occupy a special place in my heart.

To my friends and to those not so friendly. You have all made a contribution to my path. Clearly, I prefer the one made by my friends, and I will be giving each of you a squash and a squeeze in person. Thank you for tolerating my writing habit, being my cheerleaders, listening to me without trying to fix things, offering me help to get me to the finish line, and helping me celebrate every single step of my journey. There will be many more celebrations to come! I love you all.

To my clients, all the beautiful men and women who have trusted me with their truth, allowed me to reach out my hand and guide, and to those who have danced with me at my retreats. You have made a difference to my life, too, and I love you all for that. When you felt alone, you were brave enough to ask for help, and it has been the highlight of my professional life. I treasure the friendship given to me in that process.

Thank you, too, to the coaches and mentors over the years who have healed, taught, guided, inspired and challenged me, minus the dancing, sadly. Thank you for allowing me to use your stories.

To my test readers, Galia, Kate, Emma, Sarah, Mandy, Elena and Lou. Thank you for your honest, thoughtful feedback. It has shaped the book that you now hold in your hands. I was terrified to hand it over to you, and my heart is still warm from your praise.

To Jacqueline, for being everything I want to be when I grow up: elegant, eloquent, funny and honest. Thank you for taking the time to support me and write my foreword. There is no one else I would have wanted to advocate for the women who want to do more and be more without having to give up anything in the process.

To my advance reviewers, Nikki, Orla, Vanessa and Clare. Thank you for your kindness and your support. I'm so glad you liked the book and could see the impact it would have even before the professionals got their hands on it. Your input will make a huge difference, I'm sure.

To Lucy McCarraher, for *A Book of One's Own*, which I read in bed on the day before my forty-fourth birthday. That was the turning point, the moment when I said I would do this before I hit forty-five. And here I am, doing it. Thank you for your perspective. You are a constant voice in my head making all those dramatic moments completely normal. Thank you for seeing, provoking and caring for my inner rebel. Who even knew she existed? Probably everyone except me, now that I think about it!

To the Rethink Press team – Kathy, Cat, Anke, Joe and Lucy – thank you for going with and sticking to my slightly aggressive timetable. I am so glad you understood my urgency, given the time in which this book is being published. Thank you for understanding perfectly what I had in mind for the book cover and for editing down my verbosity when needed. It's been a nerve-wracking and exciting journey – just the kind I strive to be on.

And finally, to you, dear reader. Let's do this. Enough of the waiting around for people to go before us. Now is your time. Take it. You have everything you need – and more with the help of this book. If you'd like a chat one day, you know where I am. I'd love to connect.

Susie x

The Author

Susie Ramroop is a mind-set coach and international speaker. She qualified as a performance coach in 2006 while directing product development teams in the telecoms sector. She studied coaching to enhance her leadership style, but her training helped her to realise that capability and joy were not the same thing – on reaching the top of her game, she felt flat. And so she began to search for a career with more purpose. She explored teaching and healthcare transformation before deciding to focus solely on making a difference to the leaders of the future. She empowers people to take the time to know themselves, to show true leadership before they get the title, and to unlock the path to bigger, more impactful work.

Nothing gets past Susie – she sees all of your brilliance and will call out your limiting behaviour so that you surrender chuckling. Susie is an articulate and empowering coach, who brings laser focus and an enormous heart to lasting business and personal growth.

As the UK's thought leader on impostor syndrome, Susie is an exciting and, occasionally, hilarious international speaker who will have you raring to take action that makes an impact.

Susie works privately with individuals and mastermind groups in business, and runs utterly transformational retreats several times a year. She is a regular parenting contributor to *Families* magazine and BBC radio, and is often on stage at women in business and tech conferences.

Contact

✉ susie@susieramroop.com

⊕ www.susieramroop.com

▣ www.linkedin.com/in/susie-ramroop-mindset-coach

▣ www.facebook.com/coachsusieramroop

▢ www.instagram.com/susieramroop

🐦 https://twitter.com/susieramroop

⊕ www.susieramroop.com/udemy

✿ #betheleaderyouwanttosee

Lightning Source UK Ltd.
Milton Keynes UK
UKHW020006240620
365465UK00011B/334

9 781781 334591